First Lines

First published 2014 by Gazelle Press Limited

Gazelle Press

Images copyright of Staffordshire Regiment Museum, Joss Musgrove Knibb, Tamworth Herald, The Landor Society and Stoke-on-Trent City Archives. Text copyright Gazelle Press Limited.

ISBN 978-0-9930574-0-3

© Gazelle Press Limited
Printed in United Kingdom.
e-mail: gazette@hotmail.co.uk

Designed by Pebbles Design Agency
pebblesdesignagency@hotmail.co.uk

Cover image:
Men of the 1/6th North Staffordshire Regiment. May 1915.
© Staffordshire Regiment Museum.

About the author

Joss Musgrove Knibb is the deputy editor of the Lichfield Gazette and Chase Gazette Magazines. Her work has appeared in both the national and regional press and she is regularly invited to deliver talks and lectures on Staffordshire history subjects across the region.
Joss lives in Lichfield with her family.

I'LL DREAM OF YOU (2).

I'll dream of you, you dream of me, then lonely we can never be,
Fond memories my whole life long shall blend themselves in one
sweet song,
It may be me, it may be you, will miss the joys that once we knew,
So gaze towards God's sky so blue, and pray for me—I'll pray
for you.

SONG 1s. 6D.   PUBLISHED BY THE LAWRENCE WRIGHT MUSIC CO., 8, DENMARK ST., W.C.
BAMFORTH. COPYRIGHT.

Bamforth song card. The Bamforth song card series of postcards featured the lyrics of popular songs alongside an evocative image.

First Lines

The gripping letters, stories and first-hand accounts of four Staffordshire Regiment men serving in the trenches of WW1

Containing the letters of

Sergeant Sydney Norton of Tamworth

&

Sergeant James Stevenson of Stoke-on-Trent

An account by
Captain Reginald Armes of the 1914 Christmas Truce

&

The first-hand account of
Second-Lieutenant Alfred Bull of Lichfield

Joss Musgrove Knibb

Contents

Foreword

There seem to be two very entrenched schools of thought on the necessity of WW1. After the Armistice in 1918, generally expressed opinion was that it was an unpleasant job, honourably done - that the war was a necessary evil. From the late 1920s onwards the "lions led by donkeys" school of thought gained precedence, with its assertion that the war had been a pointless and criminal waste of life promulgated by backward, Victorian thinking. To my mind, the fact that the war rumbled into life again in 1939, effectively re-fighting the same territorial war (with the added impetus of an unpleasant Nazi ideology) means that WW1 was indeed necessary, if only necessitated by the land-grabbing mentality of a few.

There's also two disparate schools of thought on what experiencing that war was like for the men who actually fought it. Some imagine it as a bloody, excrement smeared hell populated by mad men, others as just another hard soldiering job, carried out by stoical, pragmatic realists, and that in addition some wartime experiences could actually be enjoyable. The letters contained in this book suggest that in fact the war could be all of these - exciting, boring, hellish, comical, utterly destructive or character building depending on the personality, and in many cases chronological age of each writer.

Living this kind of life eventually changed the way that you saw the world, literally. Like a cat, your vision would become highly attuned to movement. You would develop the capacity to sleep through thunderous noise, but wake in an instant if something in that noise threatened danger. Men who had been in the trenches for a long period learned to feel exposed and vulnerable in open spaces. They took home with them the knowledge of how easily life can be snuffed out and the grim realities of death and decomposition. It must have been almost impossible to go home and pick up where you left off if you were carrying around in your head images of the bloody deaths of friends and comrades. WW1 removed the comfortable lies that we tell ourselves to smooth over the reality of death and disease. There is no glory in a battlefield death, only the terrible fragility of flesh. Syd, James, Jake and Alfred counteract this with the kind of irreverent humour that still raises a smile a century later.

The letters and accounts included in this book are by four men who all served in the Staffordshire Regiment during WW1. They are part of the remarkable archive of letters, images and documents kept by the Staffordshire Regiment Museum in Whittington, Lichfield. I am very grateful to the Trustees of the Museum, the Head of

Research-Jeff Elson, the Curator-Danielle Pritchard, Museum Director-Major Jim Massey (Rtd) and lastly to Dave Shergold who has proved such an invaluable source of information and advice.

It took 18 months to bring this book together, and more than anything else I have ever written and researched, the material gathered here created a strange illusion of time travel. Most of the letters you'll read came out of their archive boxes in their original envelopes, complete with idiosyncratic handwriting, spelling and punctuation, and often on rain-drenched paper that made it difficult to decipher. Like the letters of any friend however, I soon got used to the syntax and foibles of each writer. It's been a conscious decision not to edit or correct any original document. They are presented here as they were originally intended to be read.

It was usual for me to transcribe one letter a day, and this simple practice of reading the thoughts of Syd, James, Jake and Alfred, day by day, effectively telescoped time. To me, these men were alive and in France. It is the remarkable ability of such letters to build bonds of friendship with strangers living a century after they were written, and if you read this book in the same way, you'll experience this. Each letter displays a lot about the character of the writer, perhaps more than many who called the authors friends would have known. Emotions are real and sometimes raw.

In the latter years of the 19th century, ordinary kids attended their local school and in most cases left at around 13. At school, as part of the curriculum you were taught correct forms of correspondence and composition which included phrases that could be used to start and end a letter. If that pupil's employment after school didn't involve much need to formally correspond, they'd stick with these letter writing formulas in later life. This meant that working class men were more likely to start their letters with a stock phrase such as "I now take the pleasure to answer", but you'll notice that Captain Reginald (Jake) Armes, who was no doubt used to corresponding every day, didn't use any of these set phrases, he just launches straight in.

These men are utterly individual. Syd Norton is brave, irreverent and shrewd. James Stevenson is romantic, honest and courageous. Alfred Bull is enormously capable and fair and Jake Armes is a great and far-sighted communicator.

It has been a privilege to get to know them. They gave so much, in some cases they gave their lives and all of their potential for love and discovery in the time that was denied them. In others, they gave three or four years and a lifetime of peace of mind that those of us who have never seen the brutality that men can inflict on other men now enjoy. The years that they gave up for us are the building blocks of our society.

And we will remember them.
Joss Musgrove Knibb
June, 2014.

Men of the 1/6th North Staffordshire Regiment. May 1915. © Staffordshire Regiment Museum.

A Little Background Information

The men that you are about to meet live in a familiar world, but a little background information may help to understand the context of some of their conversations.

Government at home

In 1914 the country was governed by the Liberal Party under Herbert Henry Asquith. He was a man considered to be a good peacetime administrator, but after a series of crises that looked like bad management (he is still blamed in part for the appalling loss of life at the Battle of the Somme at which his own son Raymond was killed) and a period of coalition government, he resigned in 1916. He was replaced by fellow Liberal David Lloyd George.

Asquith was against the Women's Suffrage Movement (Votes for Women). The struggle was building in intensity in the run up to the war, but as soon as war was declared a hiatus was called. Suffragettes and non-political women were soon to be found in hospitals and factories, driving buses and ambulances and generally stepping into the empty spaces left by those who had gone to fight. Although this kind of freedom did not last after the war, it added credence to the Suffragists' claim that women could be trusted with the right to vote. In 1918 the 'Representation of the People Act' finally gave the vote to all men over 18 (before this only 2 in 3 men had the vote. Isn't that a shocking thought, that many of the men who were required to fight and die for their country were not considered good enough to have a say in who governed it!) and all women over 30 who met certain property owning criteria. In 1928 women were given the vote on the same terms as men.

So, why did WW1 break out?

The decision by Britain and her Empire to declare war on the German Empire on 4th August 1914 was taken because Germany had invaded Belgium. Britain's hand had been effectively forced as we had a treaty in place with the Belgians and had pledged to guarantee their neutrality since 1839, a few years after it gained independence from the Netherlands. It became a world war rather than a European war because the conflict involved the global empires of Britain, France and Germany. Like dominoes falling, the Ottoman Empire soon allied itself with Germany and Japan sided with Britain. Italy joined Britain soon after and of course the United States joined the war in 1917. Few countries were not involved by 1918.

The second half of the nineteenth century was notable for the rise of nationalism within Europe (something we are all too familiar with today). Both Germany and Italy had become modern nations from the forced amalgamation of smaller states.

Ethnic groups within nations were also seeking political independence, particularly the Slavic peoples. Skirmishes and demonstrations led to great tensions within the existing Austro-Hungarian Empire and the Ottoman Empire.

The expanding empires of Britain, France, Germany and Russia created international tension that almost came to war several times. Adding to the volatility of this 'powder-keg' was a growing economic and industrial rivalry.

Many nations within Europe were embracing democracy which threatened the autocratic monarchs of some European nations (including Germany). It created a degree of political instability. The concentration of so much power within a nation upon one crowned monarch made them vulnerable.

A series of rival international treaties (including our treaty with Belgium) were meant to guarantee the security of Europe. One group of treaties were dominated by Germany and the other by France and Russia. One declaration of war upon another European nation would inevitably trigger action by a host of other nations.

Britain had lived in 'splendid isolation' since the defeat of Napoleon in 1815, but after the South African War its leaders recognised it needed friends within Europe. Rivalry with Germany led to closer links with Russia and France.

The outbreak of the First World War was triggered by the assassination of the Crown Prince of Austria-Hungry by a Serbian nationalist. Austria-Hungry went to war with Serbia. Russia backed Serbia. Germany came in on Austria-Hungary's side. France came in with Russia. Germany attacked France through Belgium and so on. Although it is now known as World War One, until WW2 it was known as 'The Great War'. The name may seem unimportant but it signals that the fighting that effectively broke Germany took place on the Western Front of France and Belgium, and that was where Germany was defeated in late 1918.

The history of the Staffordshire Regiment 1705 to 1914.
The Staffordshire Regiment can trace its beginnings to the formation of a Lillingston's Regiment of Foot in 1705 at the Kings Head public house in Lichfield. The South Staffordshire and North Staffordshire Regiments were created in 1881 and in 1908 the Regiments included a Territorial Force. By 1914 both North and South Staffordshire Regiments consisted of six Battalions, two Regular, two Militia and two Territorial. The Regiment had fought in almost every war of the 18th and 19th Century involving the British Empire.

How did the Regiment change during the war?
Both the South and North Staffordshire Regiments expanded dramatically during the War, the South Staffordshire Regiment to 16 Battalions and the North Staffordshire Regiment to 19 Battalions, a total of 35 Battalions.

This expansion was instigated by the British Minister for War, Lord Kitchener, who called for volunteers in August 1914. As a result of this 2,267,000 voluntarily joined up. Kitchener had realised that to defeat Germany Britain would need a very big army and conscription was not acceptable to the Liberal Government of 1914/15. The Volunteers formed new Battalions that were added to the Regiment's Order of Battle. Some of these Battalions recruited from specific localities creating bodies similar to the famed 'Pals Battalions'.

The Germans could field an army of over five million regular army soldiers at the start of WW1. This was because Germany practised a form of National Service. We were heavily outnumbered.

The Staffordshire Regiment's Territorial Force Battalions were originally formed for home defence only. Pressure of casualties however forced a change of policy and additional Territorial Battalions were raised to serve overseas. Syd Norton is a peacetime Territorial who went to war in 1915.

Some of the new Battalions were later reorganised for Garrison duties or Pioneer and labour duties overseas.

Where did the Regiment recruit from?
The Regiment would recruit from the old county of Staffordshire, which at the time included the Black Country up to Birmingham, but volunteers were free to join any Regiment and some recruits came from further afield. Later in the war, the advent of conscription meant that soldiers could be posted to any Regiment. In 1917/18 a shortage of manpower in France meant some units were broken up and shared between other units.

How did you volunteer?
A recruit would attend an Army Recruiting Centre, which could be sited in anything from a Town Hall to a public house. Following a medical examination, the volunteer would complete an attestation form and swear an Oath of Loyalty to The Crown. The volunteer would then be posted to his unit, or sent home to await further orders.

When did conscription come in?
On 2nd March 1916 conscription was introduced. All men aged 18 to 41 years were liable, although this was later extended to an upper limit of 51 years in 1918.

Could you get out of conscription?
In 1915 you were not liable for conscription if you were married, widowed with children, serving in the Royal Navy, a minister of religion or working in one of a number of Reserved Occupations. A second Act in May 1916 extended liability for military service to married men. Men who objected to conscription could apply to a Military Service Tribunal. Men could apply for exemption on the grounds of their employment in work of national importance, business or domestic hardship, medical unfitness or conscientious objection.

How tall did you need to be to become a soldier?
At the beginning of the war a man would have to meet the Army's strict criteria to become a soldier. In 1914 a man had to be aged between 19 and 30 years (this was later extended to 35 years). Men joining the Army had to be at least 5 feet 6 inches tall

and have a chest measurement of 35 inches. By May 1915 soldiers only had to be 5 feet 3 inches tall and the age limit was raised to 40. In July the army agreed to the formation of 'Bantam' Battalions, composed of men between 5 feet, and 5 feet 3 inches in height.

The structure of the Regiment

A Regiment never fought together, it was an organisation for administration purposes only. In WW1 the fighting unit was the Battalion, usually grouped together with three other Battalions from different Regiments into a Brigade. Four Brigades made up a Division. Two or more Divisions made up a Corps. Two or more Corps made up an Army. There were five British Armies made up of over 60 Divisions on the Western Front at its peak.

In 1917 due to manpower shortages the structure was altered to three companies to a Battalion, three Battalions to a Brigade, and three Brigades to a Division.
Within a Battalion the Non-Commissioned ranks were generally:
Private
Lance-Corporal
Corporal
Sergeant (usually spelt Serjeant)
Staff Sergeant
Company Sergeant
Quartermaster Sergeant

The Commissioned Officers ranks were:
Second-Lieutenant
Lieutenant
Captain
Major
Lieutenant-Colonel

How often did the post arrive?

Mail, leave and food were the main factors that influenced the morale of the British soldier in the Great War. Post arrived very quickly and regularly on the Western Front. The Army Postal Service was responsible for mail. It was delivering 19,000 mail bags each day across the British Channel in 1917 and in the run up to Christmas of that year it delivered half a million parcels to the front. Static trench warfare on the Western Front meant that a comprehensive network of transport for the mail was established which lasted for most of the war. Mail was usually sent up with the ammunition which indicates its high priority. 114 million parcels were distributed during the war by the Army Postal Service, most of these were parcels sent by soldier's families.

When did the Postal Morale Survey happen and what did it find out?

The morale of British troops was checked during the war by means of examining the contents of soldier's letters. On 13th September 1917 a 'Note on the morale of British troops in France disclosed by censorship' was submitted to the British Cabinet. It was based on a sample of 4,552 'Green Envelopes'. Only 28 letters or 0.61% of the sample contained any expression of complaint or war weariness. Another report to the Cabinet from the Chief of the Imperial General Staff in December 1917 based on the letters of 17,000 fighting (front line troops) over a three month period found that morale was sound.

NOTHING is to be written on this side except the date and signature of the sender. Sentences not required may be erased. If anything else is added the post card will be destroyed.

I am quite well.

~~I have been admitted into hospital.~~

~~{ sick } and am going on well.~~

~~{ wounded } and hope to be discharged soon.~~

~~I am being sent down to the base.~~

I have received your { letter dated _____ /5
~~telegram ,, _____~~
~~parcel ,, _____ /5~~

Letter follows at first opportunity.

~~I have received no letter from you~~
~~{ lately.~~
~~{ for a long time.~~

Signature }
only. } *Syd*

Date _____ *Aug 19 /15*

[Postage must be prepaid on any letter or post card addressed to the sender of this card.]

(C5540) Wt.W3497-293 1,130m. 6/15 M.R.Co.,Ltd.

An Army Form A2042 postcard completed by Syd Norton on August 19 1915. From the collection of the Staffordshire Regiment Museum. These postcards were also sometimes referred to as 'whizz-bangs', the same nickname given to a type of shell. Perhaps they were so named as they could drop through your letterbox and depending on the message they carried, deliver another kind of bombshell.

How did soldiers write home?

There were several ways…

A soldier could use a specially designed printed postcard (Army Form A2042) which listed statements like 'I am quite well' or 'I am in hospital'. He could delete that which did not apply. This meant that censorship was not required and therefore it would not be delayed. Other mail such as ordinary postcards, letters and parcels could all be sent although these were subject to censorship, usually undertaken by the soldier's Officer.

A letter could be posted in a 'Green Envelope' (Army Form 3078) which allowed the writer to sign a declaration stating that the contents contained nothing secret. Each soldier was allowed a few a week although these Green Envelopes were still liable to be checked by a Base Censor. For a soldier, postage was always free of charge.

How did it get posted?

Unit Postal Orderlies were responsible for distributing mail to soldiers. The soldier posted his mail via an Officer if it was liable to censorship, or sent it on its way himself via the supply chain to a 'Field Post Office'. The Field Post Office was a heavy black iron box under the care of a Corporal and two Sappers. It contained postal orders, stamps, cash, lead seals, rule books and so on - all that would be required to run a small Post Office. This box could be positioned anywhere, in a field, a barn, a tent, a dug out or perhaps in the Grand Salon of a Chateau. Wherever it was, this became the Field Post Office.

Two of our writers, Syd Norton and James Stevenson are Sergeants, so what was a typical day for a Sergeant in the trenches?

A Sergeant in the front line was responsible for a Platoon or a Section of soldiers and would follow a routine.

1. 'Stand to' - At an hour before dawn (the most likely time for an enemy attack) he would ensure that his men had fixed bayonets and were ready to repel an attack. This could be followed by the 'morning hate' - rapid fire in the direction of the enemy.
2. He would organise and supervise breakfast and weapon cleaning followed by a weapons inspection. This period would often include a foot-health inspection to prevent and spot 'trench foot'.
3. Allocation of Duties - The Sergeant would ensure that each soldier was given a task such as trench repair, sandbag filling, ration carrying etc.
4. The possibility for movement during daylight hours was very restricted with little activity taking place other than Sentry Duty. Most activity took place in the hours of darkness when the chances of enemy observation were reduced. Much of the time a soldier spent in a front line trench was very quiet and in fact boring. It was up to a Sergeant to keep his men alert but also rested.
5. 'Stand to' – At dusk.
6. At night the trenches came alive. A Sergeant would supervise and direct patrolling, construction and repair of fortifications.
7. A Sergeant was responsible for maintaining discipline in the front line and for setting and maintaining standards. Often

this would be achieved by force of personality as much as reliance on his rank. Much discipline was enforced informally, although it was very strict.

How often would they bathe? How often would they change clothes or clean their teeth?

A soldier's health in a front line trench was constantly at risk from the physical conditions they had to endure. In addition to the fact that the enemy were out to kill or maim, a soldier had to endure mental strain, diseases, dietary deficiencies, vermin infestations, appalling smells and all the other horrors of living in dirty conditions, around the clock and in all seasons and weathers.

Good personal hygiene could ameliorate some of this risk but the opportunities to keep clean were limited. Soldiers in the front line were subject to foot inspections and encouraged to shave. Bathing in the trench was not possible and there were no changes of uniform available. Boots could not be removed for any period of time. 'Improvised' uniform (begged, borrowed or sent from home) was allowed in very cold or wet conditions. The Army made great efforts to provide at least one hot meal a day but basic rations were not fresh and were very monotonous. Each soldier carried his own personal kit which included a shaving kit, toothbrush and sewing kit. If a soldier neglected his appearance or health this would be picked up by his NCO or Officer.

How did you go to the loo? Was there loo paper available?

A proper latrine was dug wherever possible. In poor weather, heavy fighting or if the land had a high water table this often became impossible.

Loo paper (individual squares sold in packets) was available but it is unclear if it was provided by the Army or sent from home. It was certainly used as there are instances of unofficial diaries being recorded on sheets of loo paper by British soldiers.

What happened when someone died in the trench? When and where would they be moved?

If a soldier was wounded and evacuated to a Casualty Clearing Station where he later died he would be buried at that location. There are large and small cemeteries dotted across the Western Front that are on the site of these Clearing Stations. If a soldier was killed in action in No-Man's-Land he would be unlikely to be buried. If he died in an area controlled by the Germans he might be buried in a mass grave and his details sent to the Red Cross.

If a soldier died in a front line trench during a time of heavy fighting it is unlikely he would be buried. Often his corpse would be mutilated or buried by shell fire. If it was left unburied it would decompose. Many soldiers were not buried until after the war ended and many as a result could not be identified. They have unknown graves. Soldier's burials when they did occur generally took place where they fell.

What kind of kit would an ordinary soldier carry?

The amount of kit a soldier carried depended on his role and the period of the war. The standard front line rifleman carried a weapon, usually a Short, Magazine, Lee Enfield bolt action rifle (SMLE). All the rest of the soldier's kit would be distributed around his 1908 pattern webbing ideally made of canvas but quite often made of leather. (All of Kitchener's Army were issued with leather webbing and the soldiery hated it. It was slippery and difficult to handle when wet. It also marked them out as 'new' soldiers, as the Regular Army carried canvas webbing. It was swapped, begged and borrowed whenever possible). They would carry about 150 rounds of .303 ammunition for this weapon in pouches. Attached to this webbing would be his water bottle, entrenching tool, mess tin and bayonet in a scabbard. In his backpack he would carry his Iron (emergency) Rations and a holdall also known as a 'housewife'. This cloth holdall would contain really useful items like a shaving brush and cut-throat razor, a fork and spoon, a toothbrush and a button stick. The soldier would carry a field-dressing in his inside tunic pocket (so that if possible he could dress his own wound). He would also carry his official papers, his pay book and his identity disc.

In the latter years of the war he would also carry a gas mask and several Mills bombs (hand grenades). Some men would also be responsible for rifle grenades and a Lewis gun (automatic rifle). Stokes mortars would also be carried during an attack along with communication wire, barbed wire, wire cutters and empty sandbags. Some personal items such as photographs and letters were carried. Diaries and cameras were not allowed.

North Staffords bombers on the Western Front wearing early gas hoods. Image from the collection of the Staffordshire Regiment Museum. © Staffordshire Regiment Museum.

What supplies would a soldier need to buy or have sent from home?

In the early years of the war soldiers requested two main types of item from home - special foods to supplement their monotonous diet and items of clothing for wet and cold weather. In the latter part of the war these items were not required as they became supplied by the Army or provided in canteens run behind the front lines. The Army was keen for this to happen to reduce the volume of parcels being sent. Tobacco and cigarettes were always available to soldiers. Alcohol could be bought by soldiers in Rest Areas behind the front line although it was strictly controlled in an attempt to reduce drunkenness. A tot of rum was provided in the front line in a daily 'rum ration'. It was one of the small pleasures that enlisted men looked forward to.

If you were ill, who did you see and where did you go?

Each Battalion had a Medical Officer (MO). Under the control of the Medical Officer were a party of Stretcher Bearers. There were considerable shortages of Medical Officers due to casualties and age and fitness restrictions. Also, incredibly, many felt that they were under-employed within a Battalion and tried to get posted to hospitals. From 1917 many of these Medical Officers were posted United States Army Officers. A soldier would report to his Medical Officer if he felt unwell. The MO would usually be just behind the front line but still essentially part of the unit.

What were hospitals called? What were nurses and doctors called?

Doctors and nurses were part of the Royal Army Medical Corps. The Royal Army Medical Corps (RAMC) were responsible for the…
1. Preservation of a soldier's health.
2. Treatment and care of sick and wounded soldiers.
3. Rapid collection and evacuation of the sick and wounded.

The sick and wounded were first taken to Unit Aid Posts near the front line. Field ambulances would then take soldiers to Advanced Dressing Stations where emergency operations could be carried out. There were also Divisional Collecting Stations where walking wounded could be directed.

The more seriously wounded were then taken to Clearing Hospitals (later called Casualty Clearing Stations as already discussed) or an ambulance train. From here they could be taken to Stationary Hospitals situated on the lines of communication or General Hospitals at Base or in Britain. They were transported by hospital ambulance, barge, train or ship.

Army Doctors were Officers and therefore called Sir. Nursing staff were initially provided by the Queens Alexandra's Imperial Military Nursing Service (QAIMNS) and by civilian hospitals. These were then supplemented by tens of thousands of young women who volunteered through the Voluntary Aid Detachment (VADs) and members of the First Aid Nursing Yeomanry (FANYs).

A quick note on the layout of this book

As you read the letters and accounts of Syd, James, Jake and Alf, you'll notice that scattered throughout the text are small green numbers. These correspond to explanatory notes that you'll find at the end of each piece.

Funny and sometimes obscene, British soldiers' songs was able to find humour in very grim circumstances.

I don't want to join the Army

I don't want to join the army,
I don't want to go to war.
I'd rather hang around Piccadilly underground,
Living off the earnings of a lady typist.
I don't want a bayonet in my belly,
I don't want my b****cks shot away.
I'd rather stay in England, in merry merry England,
And fornicate this bleeding life away.

Men of the 1/6th South Staffords in the Ypres salient. © *Staffordshire Regiment Museum.*

The Letters of Sergeant Sydney Norton of the 1st/6th North Staffordshire Regiment

Syd Norton was born in 1884 and was 31 years old at the time that he wrote these letters. Syd was a brewery worker who lived with his wife Fanny and their children Ethel, Arthur and Hilda. Syd had two brothers, Jack and Caleb, who were also in the Staffordshire Regiment. Jack's wife Nell lived at home with her father-in-law. Syd was a Territorial before the war, and as such was in demand as his Army training made him a capable man. In 1915 Syd was in the 1st/6th Battalion of the North Staffordshire Regiment. As you can hear from Syd's letters, he is fighting amongst a group of men who he knew well, may have gone to school with and certainly worked alongside, giving us a picture of how entire communities of men were now in France.

In the 1911 census, Syd (then 27), his wife Fanny (then 30) and their three children Arthur (5), Ethel (2), and Gladys Hilda (9) are all living at 8 Bolebridge Street, Tamworth. Syd and Fan have been married for six years. Gladys (known as Hilda) is listed as a step-daughter, so Fan must have been married, or had Hilda before she married Syd. Syd is employed as a brewer's labourer. An interesting point to note is that Fanny, her son with Syd (Arthur) and Hilda were born in Wilnecote, Warwickshire, but Syd and Ethel were born in Tamworth. Syd

Sergeant Sydney Norton

and Fanny must therefore have been living in Wilnecote at least five years before, suggesting that they were probably living with Fanny's family, a very common step at the time between getting married and getting your own place.

We join him here a short while after he has first arrived in France…

11

Presentation of a boxing trophy. Syd is in the second row, third from the left. © Staffordshire Regiment Museum.

23/03/15

Dear Wife,

Just a line in answer to your letter + Parcel I received safe, it was a bit knocked about but what was inside was alright and I enjoyed it immensely especially the apples + cake, it was a good luxury out hear after being on biscuits + bully beef, you don't wonder not passing men who have bad teeth for you want all your facilities out hear [1] Dear I have had the experience of being in the trenches. I've been in 3 days + nights – came out alright, you can hear the Germans quite plain so you can tell how close we are as they put us amongst the regulars and that's made it a lot better for us [2], shall be glad when it's all over as I am beginning to lose weight. You ask me about your letters, no, they don't look at yours. Dear we have had two casualties whilst we were in the trenches, one killed and one slightly wounded, they don't come from Tam and I've seen several popped over + they are awful sights all through being a bit brave. [3] Dear I am pleased to hear they are going on alright your way, remember me to them all hoping to see them soon if I have any luck + I dropped Jimmy Sewell a P.C last week did he get it alright. I shall write to Mr Walker this weekend, remember me to him if you see him. I shall have something to tell him about when I come over. I think this will be all this time, hoping to hear from you soon. From your loving husband Syd X Fan xxx for the children xxxxx So God Bless you all till we meet again.

P.S. Caleb has seen Bert Shelton out here, I was out when he came should have liked to have seen him, tell Mrs Shelton.
P.S. I have just received the papers, with thanks.

Bolebridge Street as it is today. Number 8 (with the black awning) is now a fashion boutique

In his letters, Syd seems pleased that a little had been taken 'off the top' of No.8. The house today is indeed two stories lower than its neighbour.

23.3.15

Dear Wife

Just a line in answer to your
Letter + Parcel I received safe it was a
bit knocked about but what was inside
was alright and I enjoyed it immensly
espeacially the apples + cake it was a good
Luxury out hear after being on biscuits +
bully Beef you dont wonder not Passing men
who have bad teeth for you want all your
faciltties out hear Dear I have had the ex-
perinces of being in the trenches Ive been in
3 days + nights came out alright you can
hear the Germans quite Plain so you can tell
how close we are they Put us amongst the
regulars and thats made it a lot better for us
shall be glad when its all over for I am begining
to lose weight. you ask me about your letters
no they dont look at yours Dear we have
had two casulties whilst we were in the trenches
one killed and one slightly wounded they dont
come from I am + Ive seen several Popped
over + they are awful sights all through being
a bit brave Dear I'm Pleased to hear
they are going on alright your way remember
me to them all hopeing to see them soon
if I have any luck & I drop Jimmy Sewell

14

Notes.

1. Syd is talking here about the effect that 'Iron Rations' had on men's teeth. 'Iron Rations' were small packages of hard biscuits and tinned 'bully' or corned beef that each soldier carried in case of an emergency. It was common for soldiers to be cut off from their usual food supplies, and a soldier's Iron Rations were just enough to keep him going for a couple of days. Syd talks about men having bad teeth as they may have had to gnaw on these rock hard 'Iron Ration' biscuits, chipping and dislodging teeth already weakened by trench life. The biscuits were designed to be dissolved in hot water, but in dangerous conditions lighting a fire to heat water would have been extremely hazardous. By all accounts, the gloop made from these biscuits was pretty inedible stuff. The average soldier would also have eaten a lot of Maconochie which was a kind of tinned stew, plus lots of bread, tinned butter and jam. Unsurprisingly, scurvy was still an issue in 1914. There would often be an unspoken truce at breakfast time as tired men sat down for a few moments with a mug of tea.

Ordinarily, it was the aim that each soldier should get at least one hot meal brought up from behind the lines each day. In addition to that, men would occasionally cook something up for themselves in the trench or would share in the food parcels sent from home. Accompanying a Regiment would be a whole selection of background services, each with their own transport. 'Cookers' were kitchen carts or lorries that held a basic oven etc. and could feed an army on the go. Sadly they were heavy and very slow, so often weren't there when the food was needed.

2. Syd is an experienced Territorial Sergeant. Territorial Battalions were made up of men who were 'part time' soldiers, working in civillian jobs for most of the year, but also training as soldiers in reserve. Hence, when Syd was called up he was a brewer, but also already an experienced Sergeant and a useful man to have around. Here, Syd is talking about his Territorial Battalion being in the trenches alongside regular soldiers (full-time, long-term soldiers). It would have helped the Territorial Battalion get to grips with trench etiquette and behaviours faster, and that could save your life.

3. Every day the Officer in charge of each section was required to write up the day's events in a War Diary. These diaries are held at the Staffordshire Regiment Museum and consistently back up Syd's letters.

6th South Staffordshire Regiment 'cookers' behind the lines. © Staffordshire Regiment Museum.

4/4/15

Dear Wife

Just a line in answer to your 2 parcels and letter I have received, I can't make it out about you not having received any reply for I wrote straight away a week last Tuesday, there are several chaps in the company have wrote several letters home and they have not had them, theres some delay somewhere for I hope you get this letter alright, for they are allowing Sergts one of these envelopes once a week, so its making it a bit better for sending home [1]. You ask me about the letters you send me, well they don't censor yours nor look at them, so you need not be afraid to put anything in, so don't put anything rude in for we are very modest sorts of chaps out here especially now I am beginning to pick a bit of French up and we have had a short address from the Bishop of London and been inspected by Gen French and several big Generals, and have had the experience of being in the trenches right close up to the Germans, you can hear them singing and playing a Brass Band all night long. I was put in with the Welch Fusiliers and I enjoyed it very much. We were under very heavy shell fire the last day I was in, there was not much damage done as our artillery soon quietened them all, as we have to do, keep your head low if you don't (it's get out and get under) for their snipers are demons [2] and you can't find them that's the most trouble to our troops and we only lost one killed and one wounded out of our Rgt and have seen several knocked over and they are not very pleasing sights I can tell you, but you don't have to show any sympathy out on this job, and we are about to go in the trenches again, we have been out for a rest. We have to go in for 5 days and come out for 5, the only danger is going in and out and I shall be glad when it's all over and you will I know, and what sort of an Easter are you having, it don't seem like holiday time here. I had a letter from Eva, she said she was coming over to spend Easter with you all. We marched in a large town and spent Good Friday, we enjoyed ourselves as well as we could. We had a good look round at the sights, the place was packed, all sorts of troops and we were billeted in an asylum, well you should have heard the remarks passed and then we had a walk round the burial ground, a sight I don't want to see again, so that's how I spent my holidays and now we are in huts in Belgium and our troops are pushing well forward and instead of the Germans chasing us, we are chasing them. Dear you need not send the News of the World, there are several papers we get here on Mondays and I have read them by when I get yours, and I notice they charge you plenty to send a parcel out here, but if you put on the bottom of the address (C/O Forwarding Dept, Southampton), they will come a bit cheaper. Dear, I was wondering about that photo, they have told us they had sent one to our homes and you would have to forward the money if satisfied with the photo, so I will leave it with you what to do but I hope to have the pleasure to see one in my (serious) position [3]. Dear, did you touch the winner of the big events [4] and is your Dad having any luck, hoping he is and is your mother going on alright and remember me to Nell and dad, hoping they are going on alright and you have been having nice weather, we have been enjoying nice sunshine but very cold nights but I have been pretty comfortable in barns, plenty of straw to lay on but not like the feather bed I have left behind, and my dutch [5] and (little grey home in the west) but what a day it will be when we do meet once again for ever, looking forward to another 10 years happiness better than the past. Dear, I have received the Easter Eggs alright [6]. I think this will be all this time, hoping you will get this letter alright for I feel a bit savage about you not getting the last letter but you may have received it by when you get this, finding you all in the best of health and hoping the children are going on alright, kiss them all for me. I shall be pleased when I can give them all a real one and likewise yourself and many a thousand beside. We shan't half smack one another and make up for lost time what do you say Dear keep smiling from your ever loving Husband Syd X Fan xxxxx For the Children xxxxx God Bless them.

P.S. You might send a few Beechams Pills [7] the next time you send. I have plenty of envelopes + writing paper.

Syd's letter of 4 April 1915. Document from the collection of the Staffordshire Regiment Museum.

Notes

1. The envelopes Syd mentioned were known as 'Greenies' (see image). They were envelopes that put the soldier on his honour not write anything in a letter that could be used to glean information by the enemy. They were not read by one of the Officers, as ordinary letters were meant to be. In reality, very few letters were ever read and censored. There were too many other pressing jobs to attend to.

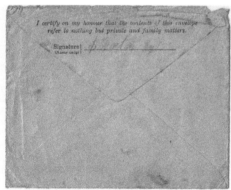

A Green Envelope (Army Form 3078) known as a 'Greenie' would put the writer on their honour not to include anything within it that could give useful information to the enemy. Documents from the collection of the Staffordshire Regiment Museum.

2. There were several things that needed to become second nature. Syd talks about 'get out and get under', this meant to keep your head down below the top of the parapet. It was important to only use the Trench Binoculars (a kind of periscope) to view activity in No-Man's-Land, popping your head up for a look was suicide. It was also important to become familiar with the sound of the 'outgoing' and 'incoming' artillery rounds of your own side and that of the Germans

3. This would have been either a group photograph taken of Syd's Company, or perhaps just one of Syd and his mates taken by an enterprising local photographer that was available for families back home to buy. Syd would like to see a picture of himself as a Sergeant in wartime.

4. In other words, did you put a bet on a big horse race and win?

5. 'Dutch' is one of Syd's pet names for his wife. It may well have been inspired by a popular Music Hall song "My Old Dutch" that has the line "There ain't a lady livin' in the land, as I'd swop for my dear old Dutch". 'Dutch' is thought to be short for Duchess.

'My Little Grey Home in the West' was also a popular song of the time.

6. These Easter Eggs would have been made of chocolate.

7. Beechams Pills were laxatives, and unlike many other medicines at the time they did work. They were also supposed to have a generally restorative effect on the digestive system, hence this ad from 1915 (see page 21) that is a double entendre that refers both to a man passing the tests to join up (and moving his bowels) first time due to the remarkable effect of Beechams Pills. As you can see, he wears a Military Armband, signifying he has just joined the Army (men who were waiting to receive orders would wear this armband, to avoid being labelled cowards).

LITTLE GREY HOME IN THE WEST (1).

When the golden sun sinks in the hills,
  And the toil of a long day is o'er—
Though the road may be long, in the lilt of a song
  I forget I was weary before.

Bamforth song-card. My Little Grey Home in the West.

Newspaper advertisement for Beecham's laxative pills.

21

11/04/15

My Dearest Wife,

In answer to your welcome and loving letter I received last Saturday, pleased to hear you are all going on alright as it leaves me the same at present, as we have had rather a rough time since I had your last letter, we had orders to move out of the huts Easter Monday night into the trenches, it was pouring down a rain all day and we had to stand nearly an hour before we made a shift and then marched 6 miles simply wet through and then we were put into a barn and had to lay in our clothes till it got daybreak, expecting an attack but it did not come off, a good job for us it didn't, if they had done they could have wiped us out with a big stick we were about done up, never have I experienced such a time, there were bullets and shells all directions flying about and we have lost 3 more men killed including a Sergt and 2 wounded not out of our Company yet but I didn't go into the trenches. I had a worse job that I have had in my life behind the trenches burying dead cows, horses and pigs what's been dead for months, fair rotten, but the worst about it we had to go out at ten o'clock at night till 2 in the morning, pitch dark and raining all the time crawling about on hands and knees till we could find them bullets flying over our heads but the stench was awful and then we found three dead bodies, 2 English and 1 Frenchman to finish up with of course it did not affect me much it was the men under me. [1] The biggest trouble I had to tell them they had got to do it or get shot at dawn, I loaded my rifle that was enough, of course I was only pulling their leg, of course as I have said you don't have to show any sympathy out here when you are put a job to do it's got to be done without any back chat, and when I got back safely and the men, I felt a bit sick with the stench on my stomach, we had some pills and then a hot bath and I began to feel in the pink again (not half) we have arrived back for a rest for 5 days and then we go back again and the villages we march through, it's awful and a cruel sight what the Germans have done indescribable [2]. Jack went into the trenches I expect he will tell Nell all about it he don't care much about it nor nobody else when they are close to them, they were only 80 yds from the Germans. Dear Fan I received Arthur's photo it's a very good one of him the little swank wore his stripes, it's about time he had one I see he has got my swagger [3] tell him to take care of it till I come over and I'm glad to hear you enjoyed my letter but you would have enjoyed it better if I had been there, I hope it didn't make any extra washing for you [4]. Dear, when you send over again you might send me a towel and some emery cloth, you need not send any more cigarettes we have hundreds of them sent us and get plenty of time to smoke them and we have plenty of rum but we cannot get any beer where we are, never seen any for 8 days almost forgot the taste. I shall be teetotal when I come over, being going without so long and I think Tamworth people are a miserable lot since we have been in this country have not received a single thing not even a Herald, I don't know what we should do if it wasn't for the Lichfield Sgts people, they are sending something almost every week from Lichfield townspeople, they send them books and papers and footballs, mouth organs etc. Dear I had a box of cigarettes come the other day it was from Birmingham on the post mark there was no letter with it so I don't know who it's from I wondered if it was from one of (my old girls) (don't get your hair off) They smoke alright I think I will send you one over, and I received the papers alright also Weekly Despatch, thanking you very much and I think this will be all this time, closing with fondest love from your most ever loving husband Syd X Fan XXXX Give my love to the children tell them our general says we shall be over for June 1 hope it's for Whitsuntide he has offered anyone of us £100 if any of us capture a German dead or alive, there is one had a go at it and has not been seen since. I think I will wait a bit and see, remember me to all enquiring friends, and Jack Pickering and Harry Allsopp, ask him to remember me to Ria Sharp at the Pit when he sees him so goodnight and God Bless you all till we meet again. XXXXXXXXX Syd.

Syd's letter of 11 April 1915. Document from the collection of the Staffordshire Regiment Museum.

Notes

1. It was important to clear the bodies of dead animals from between the lines, not least for reasons of health. It seems that snipers would often crawl up to these bodies under the cover of night and use them to hide behind during daylight as they picked off men in the nearby trench. Often it was possible to collect the remains of a dozen men as a few scattered fragments of bone and flesh, and carry them down for burial on a ground-sheet.

2. There's been a lot of debate about whether stories of the atrocities laid at the door of the Germans were true, or just embroidered to fit the idea of the evil Hun.

Syd's letters suggest that the actions of the enemy on the civilian population were very disturbing.

3. Syd has just received a picture of his son Arthur (aged 9) wearing his Dad's Sergeant's stripes. It appears that he's also got his Dad's swagger stick, which was a short wooden stick that you would carry tucked under the arm.

A brief note about what a Sergeant did...A Sergeant would take orders from anyone of higher rank. Their responsibility was dependant on their specific role and posting. A Battalion of about 1,000 soldiers was divided into four Companies. Each Company of about 220 soldiers was divided into four Platoons which in turn each had four Sections. Each platoon of about 50 soldiers would have a Sergeant who would support a Junior Officer. Each Section of about 12 soldiers would be led by a Sergeant or Corporal. Of course with soldiers being killed, wounded, away on leave or on training courses these numbers were often much lower.

4. Syd is either referring to his wife shedding tears, or is being very suggestive indeed!

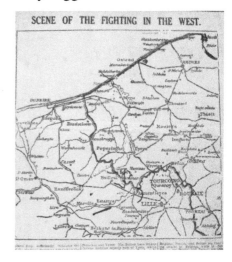

Men of the 6th South Staffordshire Regiment with carrier pigeons. Pigeons were quite extensively used as a useful method of communication. More traditional means were also used and telephones were available, however they were connected by long lengths of wire that were easily damaged.
©*Staffordshire Regiment Museum.*

SCENE OF THE FIGHTING IN THE WEST.

19th April 2015

My Darling Wife

Just a line to say I've received your loving letter and parcel alright and I've some more good news for you, I have been promoted to full Sergt dated from 1.3.15 and I've seen the Pay sergt about the back money he will put things alright, for you will hear in a week or so, and have been made senior as well, and we are doing some wonderful work and plenty of it, we have been in the trenches again and had 4 killed and 5 wounded, and had a bit of an attack on Saturday night, it only lasted about an hour, it was a grand sight from a distance, but the guns were deafening. We captured some Germans, they were in a bad condition had no food for days, our losses very slight, they said had got a lot killed, they gave themselves up, they have had enough of it [1] and when it got daybreak you could see a lot dead lying here and there. I only had one look, that was enough for me. Well we are back again for a rest thank God. I say a little prayer when we are relieved for we don't get even a wash nor a shave till we get out and we look pretty ducks and I'm feeling in the best of health now, I have had a change and a good bath so this is all I have to tell you of my rough time in the trenches. Dear I enjoyed the parcel you sent and the cigarettes I received from Brash, remember me to him when you see them, tell him I will write to him soon and sorry to hear you have had bad luck with the eggs you have experienced other years, you should get your own eggs for the future and don't bother about anyone else's, and you will have to get another cockerel if you want to do any good or wait till I come over [2] , and don't get knocked up while doing the garden, I can picture you with a shovel, you can send us a few onions if they are hot when they are up [3]. We get plenty of bread and cheese out here but I hope I am over to enjoy them with you and the old half pint like we used to have. Dear, you ask me about socks and shirts, well I have plenty of things to wear we have just had an issue of new things. I want you to get me a new pocket note book, one to put in my pocket and when you send another parcel send us a tin of milk for that's what we are very short of out here. We get plenty of tea [4] and it's as nice again, we are making tea all day long and sometimes all night especially when it's cold nights and can't go to sleep [5], and thank Mr Riley for the cigarettes and matches, hoping to see him soon, tell him I am going on alright, a bit quiet being lonely I guess, what do you say, and you might try to get some stuff to dust my shirt [6], we are beginning to find some reinforcements, we call them jaspers out here you can see the chaps busy everyday for about an hour, its lying in these barns, you can change, everything clean and you are as bad the next day, of course it finds us something to do while the shells are flying over our heads, we don't take much notice of them, we are getting used to them, take no notice and aeroplanes buzzing about all day long like flies. [7] Dear I have not heard anything about Gladys yet, you did not say how much you got on the 12th, you will be alright now, I wish I was closer we wouldn't half wet it [8], I bought a bottle of wine out here amongst us not enough to get drunk. Dear, remember me to our dad and mother, wishing them the best of wishes also dad and

Nell. We are having lovely weather out here and we are having a band playing in the afternoon, so you can see we are pretty comfortable in the rest camp but I should be more comfortable in my own rest camp. Dear I think this will be all this time give my love to the children, glad to hear that they are going on alright.

Tell Ethel I shall be over soon and tell her to get a big girl and eat plenty of pudding, hoping it will be over soon, from your ever and fondest love from your ever loving husband Syd X Fan so goodnight and God Bless you all, from Sergt, Syd XXXXXXXXXX

Notes

1. One of the most dispiriting things for a German soldier was the lack of food, both in the trench and at home. British ships were doing a very good job of blockading and destroying food cargoes bound for Germany. Soldiers at the front knew that their families were close to starving at home, in fact roughly half a million Germans starved to death in their own homes from 1914 to 1918. In addition, all German soldiers were conscripts, there was no voluntary service.

2. Fanny Norton, like most wives at the time, was also having to deal with wartime rationing. Many people grew their own food and raised their own chickens, but chickens (as Fan has just found out) don't always lay. Despite this, rationing in Britain was never as severe as it was in Germany.

3. Syd is obviously craving some hot, tangy onions to brighten up the stew, corned beef, bread, potatoes, butter, jam and eggs (in different combinations) that made up practically every meal.

4. 'Gun fire tea' was a very strong, very sweet tea made with tinned milk that had the ability to keep all but the most exhausted soldier standing. Cigarettes, tea and the daily rum ration keep the army on its feet.

5. Living in the trench in all weathers meant that you got used to doing everything outdoors including sleeping. A good spot to sleep was on the Fire Step (a raised platform that was used as a stage to fire from). It had the advantage of being raised out of the mud, water and worse that would slosh around in the trench bottom in rainy weather, or all the time if the local water-table was high. Traditionally sleeping quarters were known as 'Dug-Outs' or 'Funk Holes'. An Officer's Dug-Out could be a small room complete with bunks, tables, chairs etc dug into the walls of the trench. Equally, an Officers Dug-Out might consist of an old German trench or shell hole with a couple of sheets of corrugated iron for a roof. If it had a roof, it was prime real estate. If you were an ordinary soldier however your sleeping quarters were likely to be a hole scraped into the earth of the trench wall (either just enough for one man in which case it was known as a 'Funk Hole, or about the size of the average domestic fridge on its side). It is remarkable how many men would squeeze into this space. At least with lots of bodies it would have been warm, if malodourous. A soldier would try to grab a little sleep in whatever he was stood up in, wrapped in his great-coat or a ground sheet. There are no set rules on where to sleep so he would just curl up wherever he could, be it a shallow scrape or literally in the middle of the trench, so that others would need to step over him. Needs must. If you were in a Rest Camp or somewhere with a bit more space, you

might unroll your 'flea bag' (as the soldiers named them) or a couple of Army ration blankets. A 'flea bag' was a type of sleeping bag or bed roll that could provide a bit more comfort, and yes, they did contain fleas, lice, and anything else that was currently living on you.

6. Syd is asking for an insecticide power to treat his clothing as he, like everyone else would have suffered with body lice. Lice lived and bred on the body and clothing and washing would not kill them. You could however run a thumb nail, a candle flame or a lighter along any clothing seams to kill the eggs and adults living there (leaving a greasy smell as they died) and pick off the adults by hand. If left untreated, lice bites could turn into sores (caused by soldiers scratching the itchy bites and forcing the faeces of the louse into the open bite). These sores would then give you a condition called 'Trench Fever' that led to nausea, fever, vomiting and even death in some cases. More of this later. Syd and his mates have christened the lice 'Jaspers'. Often, men would also shave their heads as head-lice (nits) were also endemic.

7. Aeroplanes would fly over the British lines first thing in the morning, and then report back so that the gunners knew where to aim their shells. They were duly hated.

8. In other words Syd and Fan would wet their whistles with a few drinks if they were together.

A soldier of the 2nd North Staffords in a dug-out in 1916. Bayonets might be stuck into the trench wall to provide a peg from which you could hang your water bottle, or extra ammunition. Spent shell cases were often drilled through and hung up. They could be rung like a bell to warn of a gas attack. © *Staffordshire Regiment Museum.*

5.5.15

Dearest Wife,

Just a line in answer to your loving letter and parcel I received in the trenches on Sunday. I have come out to the rest camp till we go back again. I had a gruelling experience this time, I went in with 50 men who had not been in before but kept them well together. We had a lively time on Monday, the Germans started shelling our trench, they blew my dugout all to pieces and what was inside it [1]. I had just come out just before the shell did its work and I ran to see if anyone was hurt, only a sergt who was picking himself up, buried beneath some sandbags, and then our artillery started to work and blew about 80 yards of their trenches down and then my men got into another trench and started to give them their supper (Iron rations) and I went and inspected my dugout the next day, all my belongings went west. I had a mashing of cocoa and the tin of dust out of your parcel saved and myself thank God. I didn't half shake hands with myself, they sent us about 12 shells over and that was all the damage they had done. I think they had a grudge against me, for me and another sergt the day before found a sniper, we watched his antics for 2 hours and I placed a rifle at him, bowled him over the third shot and then got back to our trench, that's what we do in the day time, pick three of the best shots and go sniping, its dinking sport like looking for game, they are very smart, you can tell, we saw a dead cow in front of our trench, we fired a volley into it and the next day the scouts went out and found a dead sniper inside it so you can tell the antics of war craft they get up to and our officers have complimented us on our hard work and the way we handled the men and I told them to show good heart lads and let them have it and we came out without any casualties that's all we look for on these sorts of jobs, we came out this time without any loss, we are sorry about sergt Harper, he didn't get shot, it was hard lines, he was found choked on his back with his false teeth [2], if you see his wife you can tell her she has our deepest sympathy from the company. Dear fan I am using the dust it seems to be decent stuff, I am having a bit more peace of course, I have to persevere everyday what we call chatting [3], they take some shifting like the Germans, and I'm sorry that your mother is not so well, of course she is getting on in years and she has had a hard life and its bound to tell in old age and hope she will get better for when I come home some day, I don't know when that will be and tell your dad, thanks for the cigars I shant smoke them yet but I shall do tonight, perhaps am going down to a boozer and have an enjoyable smoke, the pubs out here are called du bossions or estaminet [4], I aint half picking the language up, I shall know my road about when I get in some big town, dear pleased you are having nice weather we are having it very hot here and will you send me some foot powder [5] when you send again and you need not send butter every time us sergts have a decent lot of butter and we are having plenty of honey amongst the jam so we are not short of food, [6] we live well in the trenches you can send us some sweets as well, dear remember me to dad and Nell, I will try to write to them soon, hoping they are going on alright and Mr. and Mrs. Walker, I wrote to them some time ago but never had any answer, I don't know whether they had it and sorry to see in the herald about Alf West's son, give them me and Caleb's sympathy and remember me to inship when you see him. Dear I think this will be all this time, hoping you will enjoy my letter and I think it's the same moon I wish me and you were under it and how are the children going on, give my love to them, God bless them. Has Arthur got a stripe yet. From your ever loving husband Syd X Fan xx for the children xxx and a sweet one for you x

Notes

1. Syd has, in other words, lost everything – food, pills, whatever he didn't carry on him.

2. It's possible that Sergeant Harper was concussed by the force of a close explosion, and choked on his own false teeth while unconscious. There were all kinds of ways you could be killed, ranging from bayoneting, stabbing and clubbing to death during a trench raid, to shooting with rifle, revolver, or machine gun, dismemberment from land mines and Mills bombs (a kind of hand grenade, you can often see them in contemporary prints, they look almost like a relay baton with a stick that is topped by a cylindrical head) or by the many and various types of shell, culminating in the terrifying 'minenwerfers', that the men called 'minnywoffers' that were 3.5 feet high and held 200lbs of explosive. The only warning that one of these monsters was arriving was the faint sound of a whistle made by the German gun crews. When it exploded it would simply scythe through everything around it, vaporising anything it came into contact with. Even if you weren't hit by a shell, the force of the blast could kill you just as easily. In addition to shells you also had to contend with poison gas. For much of the war gas was used to disrupt and incapacitate. Tear gas we are sadly familiar with today and

Mustard gas causes burns and temporary blindness that lasts for at least two weeks. Phosgene and chlorine gas however are killers. Gas was first used by the French but was quickly taken up by the Germans and British. Both phosgene and chlorine gas attack soft tissue, rendering the lungs useless. If you breathed it in you would effectively drown. It could be an instant or a long drawn out death, depending on how much you breathed in. Years after the war men were still struggling with the after-effects of gas. There was no cure. Gas masks of varying designs were distributed to the troops, including a simple canvas hood that it was first advised you should keep wet (many soldiers urinated on them) and then, in direct contradiction, advised you should keep dry. They did very little good and did not keep out the gas effectively. There was also no efficient way of firing the gas into the enemy's lines, so it was simply released when the wind was blowing in the right direction. Wind direction however can change in an instant and bring the toxic yellow miasma back to you. Soldiers also had to contend with flame throwers, dogs and some Officers who still went into battle wearing swords. However, in practice, most soldiers were killed or wounded by artillery. If you add in the common occurrences of disease and ill-health, rat bites, septicaemia from rusty

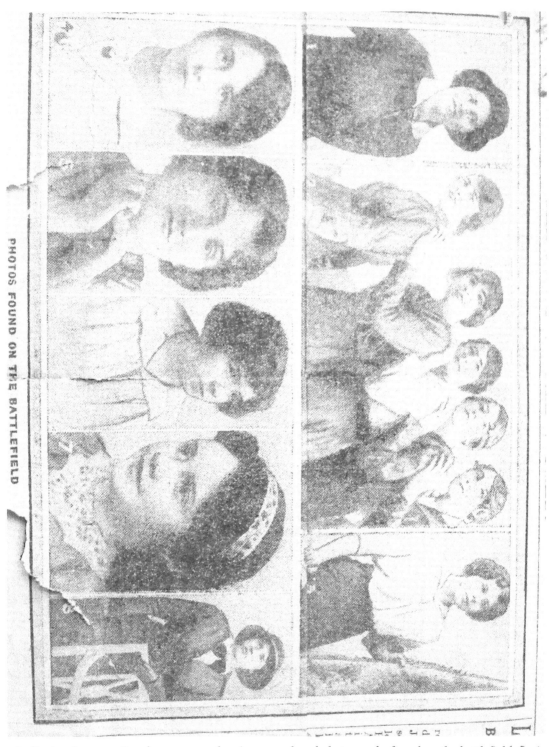

A clipping from a national newspaper showing reproduced photographs found on the battlefield. Seeing your face or that of your children in this way could often be a first, unofficial indication of widowhood. This image came from the documents pertaining to Sergeant Sidney Marsden, whose widow's foreboding that her husband was probably dead was confirmed when she saw the face of her daughter (second row, fourth from left) in her daily paper. The mundane horror of that is beyond imagining. Document from the Staffordshire Regiment Museum collection.

barbed wire and the cornucopia of other ways you could be quickly snuffed out, if you survived you were a very lucky and very tough individual indeed.

Sometimes relatives would write asking if a personal item, a ring or a watch could be returned, or enquire about money their husband might have had on them. Of course, in many cases there would not be a body to search for such things. Soldiers would routinely collect the Army Pay Books of any dead they found. All soldiers carried these and it was an ideal form of identification. As the war went on it also became common practice for photographs found scattered on the battlefield to be sent to the national newspapers. Their owners would be dead, lost in the mud or dismembered, with no other way of identification. Wives might easily see their own face, or that of their children looking at them out of the pages of the News of the World. It was an unofficial signal of widowhood.

A bone rosary containing a Stanhope.

3. This is the origin of the term 'to chat'. In the trenches soldiers would spend time delousing themselves (dusting with insecticide power, searching for lice etc.) and would talk while doing so. Lice were commonly known as chats, and had been called this since at least the 18th century. This delousing process then became known as 'chatting' and when the soldiers came home after the war the phrase passed into common usage and came to describe a group of people sitting around talking. A friend of mine recently told me that her Grandmother used to say that someone was "chatty but happy" if they were scratching an itch – A turn of phrase straight from the trenches if ever I heard one!

4. It was quite usual for soldiers to nip down to the local bar for a little rest and relaxation. Inevitably there were also many instances of prostitution as lonely men looked to spend their money on a little comfort (Bethune had a notorious red-light district).

Perhaps whilst in the bar, Syd might have bought a gift to send back home? There are many examples still existing in collections and private homes of what were essentially tourist items that soldiers bought from the locals (who made them specifically for the troops) and sent home to their wives and sweethearts. This carved bone rosary with stanhope (a stanhope is a tiny image magnified by a lens that was set into many objects of this sort) is one example of this.

5. Soldiers would be on their feet all day, and even when the weather was hot and the trenches were dry this could cause a lot of foot problems, hence Syd's asking for

talcum powder. If the weather was wet soldiers would inevitably spend hours with wet feet held in sodden boots. This caused a condition known as trench foot where the skin becomes white and spongey and eventually dies. It is remarkably painful. To counteract this regular foot inspections were put in place. Soldiers were advised to take their wet socks off every night and dry them in front of the fire, they would then grease their feet with whale oil to try and form a barrier between their skin and the moisture. 6. Ideally men would receive at least one hot meal a day that would be transported in a 'hay box'. This was a wooden box stuffed with hay that would insulate the metal cooking pot inside it that held the food. Of course, often it was spilt, or delayed and would be stone cold by the time it arrived. It could also have been dipped into several times on route so there might not have been much left by arrival!

14/05/15

My Dearest loving Wife,

In answer to your loving letter, pleased to hear you have got over your troubles and bereavement I was thinking of you all day sat and picturing you in my thoughts, I guessed you would have to do the running about and wondering if you would knock yourself up because they are big jobs [1] and hoping she has gone to a better land, of course they are not big jobs out here, if you get killed its all over in an hour there was one poor chap picked a shell up unexploded it went off in his hand and was killed instantly and was buried straight away. I attended the burial so you can see they are not long putting you out of this world. Dear, I had a bit better time in the trenches this time than I did the last time in my little dug out in the West they let us have a few shells over but did no damage they knocked one tree down behind us (of course I wasn't up the tree) and where we are it's just one ridge and you can see for miles around, the country begins to look beautiful bar the houses and churches which are in ruins and we can see more with our powerful glasses and it was that quiet at times you wouldn't think there was a war on and only a 70 yards from them but its night time when we give it one another I expect you think I am asleep at nights, that's when the dirty work has to be done. We had a fine bit of sport, we seen one of our aeroplanes bring a German aircraft down, he was chasing him for 20 minutes in the air and dodging one another till he dropped to the ground and we can hear a lot of firing on our right and left now and again and some of our chaps were talking to the enemy from our trenches the other day calling them all the names the tongue could tell and they tried to speak English as well as they can but we did not trust them, we let them have one or two rounds and quietened them.
Dear, you ask me about publishing my letters, no I don't think it's possible to, not because I am afraid, you can show them anybody, as you know I am going to write one to the board of trade to publish. I have had a letter from them, they are sending

my Platoon some cigarettes and tobacco and also I have had a letter from Mrs A. Walker and some Woodbines [2] tell her when you see them I will write soon. Dear does your Dad want to stop with you it would be company for you, of course there will be a home for him when the war is over or when I come back if he behaves himself. Dear, tell Hilda to get better for I have got a nasty tickling cough this last week I don't know how I have caught it for the weather has been awfully hot and the weather has changed this last 2 days, we are having some rain and upset all calculations and we have got Capt Jenkinson back again after his illness, he looks a lot better than he did. Did you see Caleb's letters in the Herald. Capt has wrote to Mrs Harper and how is she going on. I am glad to see you like my nice letters, I should like to put something nicer in for you for Whitsuntide, hoping you will all enjoy your-selves and have nice weather, you know what the song says (I wish I was there). Dear I think this will be all this time, remember me to Dad and Nell, give them my love and give my love and kisses to the children and God Bless them XXXXX likewise yourself, from your ever loving husband Syd X Fan XXXXX Goodnight and God Bless you Dear till we meet again.

P.S. Please send some more of this sort writing paper when you send again and some carbolic. XX.

Notes

1. Syd's mother-in-law has died. The 'big job' he's referring to is the funeral. He goes on to talk about how deaths are not marked in the trenches.

2. We now know that smoking is very bad for the health, but it's a fact that cigarettes, pipes and cigars kept the troops going during the war. Nicotine dulls hunger, calms the nerves and sharpens the mind in addition to giving just a tiny little bit of pleasure in very unpleasurable circumstances. It also gave bored or anxious men something to do and the illusion of warmth in bitter weather.

Syd's letter of 14 May 1915

33

17/5/15

Dear Wife,

Just a line to say I am going on alright hoping you all are the same. I am sending you two 5 Franc notes for you for Whitsuntide to spend on the children and yourself. You can change them at Lloyds bank and the Post Office, you will get 8/4 for them. I meant to have sent them in my last letter but quite forgot but better late than never they say. Hoping you will enjoy yourselves and have nice weather, we are having some rain just at present for it is wanted here badly, everything dried up. Dearest I hope you will get them alright let me know soon for we can't spend them where we are just at present. I hope to send you 2 more soon. All this time, love to the children and yourself, from your loving husband Syd X Fan. For the children XXXXX. God Bless you all.

9.6.15

Dear Wife,

In answer to your most welcome letter and pleased to hear you are going all alright as it leaves me the same at present, only the hot weather mawles my fat [1] its awful hot out here but I think there is going to be a change its thundering and lightening just at present. Whilst writing this letter I received the parcel alright and it just came right, we had to stop in the trenches two days longer and we had a beano on Sun for tea, we had lettuce, onion and cucumber all mixed up in vinegar, as it happened there was a lot of us had parcels and we all shared in it it was almost like being at home only for the bullets and shells whizz over your heads, we are getting used to them and take no notice of them and we have had a few more casualties we lost 2 Corps out of our Company but not from Tam, one leaves wife and 6 children and the other has his mother depends on him. I attended 2 funerals the other day and we trimmed Gadsbys and the comrade's graves and made them look nice. Dear there is a rumour going about us coming over to England about the end of this month, there is a lot of Terriers [2] come to England, there is something in it. Our 2 officers are coming over next week for 7 days from Lichfield they come from. I hope its true and we have any luck to come back for good not for 7 days, we deserve a rest, as we came out of the trenches this time we captured a spy and we pounced on him, pinned him up against a building which he was trying to get in till our officers came up and searched him it was about midnight, he has been tried twice, he is being tried again tomorrow. I think he is a German, he can't speak French or Belgian so it looks very bad for him. Dear that George Smith has been wounded him what come to our house when we came on Pass that night, he comes from Baddesley, he got shot above the knee coming out of the trench.

Dear, I hear a good account of your new Palace at Tam about, [3] they have got 6 nice chocolate girls dressed in white and that figure on the top is Mrs Dent and they say she has been bathing and lost all her clothes and Mr Jenson has gone cross eyed looking at her this is what has come from Tam to some of the boys who are with me. I have got a nice school, they read some of their letters from some of their pals to me, of course they put a bit more to it, they break their necks to tell me especially if it's about the Grand Theatre they say it's a fine place have you been yet [4]. Caleb & Jack are going on alright and pleased the children are looking so well. Tell them they won't know me when I am coming home, tell them I shall be a Frenchman (I don't think). Dear I must draw to a close, hoping I shall see you soon and the war over, getting fed up, remember me to Dad and all enquiring friends. From your most ever loving husband Syd X Fan XXXXX

For the children XXXXX

P.S. Send us some more Beechams please.

God Bless you all.

The Grand Theatre, George Street, Tamworth. Syd's comrades keep reading him extracts of their letters from home that are full of news of this new theatre and cinema. Note the scantily clad figure of Venus at the top of the facade. © The Tamworth Herald.

Notes

1. Mawles my fat, or in other words, Syd is really suffering in the heat
2. Terriers – A nickname for the Hertfordshire yeomanry / Infantry.
3. On November 1910 The Palace Electric Theatre opened on George Street, in Tamworth. The Palace was designed by Clason & Fidler, who were Tamworth architects. It put on both Music Hall acts and the occasional cinema film, so Syd would have known it well. In 1915 however it was renovated and re-named the Palace Cinema. The Palace Cinema is no longer standing, but its site is part of the Ankerside Shopping Centre on George Street.
4. Syd is talking here about The Grand Theatre, George Street, Tamworth, which was owned by Charles H Dent and again put on both Music Hall and cinema films. It opened its doors on 19th May 1915 and could seat 700 people in grand style. It had an orchestra pit and balcony and a stage that was around 18 feet wide, below it were dressing rooms for the acts. Its frontage was finished in red brick and terracotta and was crowned with a statue of a semi-clad Venus. It closed in 1958 and was demolished. The site is now shops and offices.

It seems that Syd is getting confused reports from his mates' letters, as he puts the statue of Venus (that Syd jokes is Mrs Dent) from the Grand Theatre on top of the Palace Cinema instead! Chocolate girls were usherettes in smart uniforms who sold chocolates from a tray to the audience in the intervals.

4.7.15 (Sunday)

My Dear Wife,

In answer to your loving letter I received on Sat and the parcel I received on Thurs which was very acceptable and thanks for the bottle of (pick me up) [1] it comes in handy on a morning for its very cold out in the open. I drink it neat for we can't get any out here where we are and we keep moving about from one place to another and its very hot in the daytime and we are at a very pretty place right in the country amongst the cornfields not far from the firing line and we have had a good spell out of the trenches, have not been in for a fortnight but we have had plenty to do and we go in again on Monday night for 6 days close to Ypres. I have been through that place once, I had to go with 50 men to make a trench and they started shelling us and we had to lie down in one of the streets for an hour I thought our time had come but we kept calm till they had finished but we got through alright without any casualties and it's a big fine place, almost as big as Birmingham big mansions all been hit with shells [2]. I had a look in one, there was the most beautiful furniture I have seen. Pianos and organs and splendid clocks all left behind, not a living soul in the place, rows of houses just the same and just before I left I was shown a big Brewery where they captured 200 Germans all drunk, the Scots captured them and they didn't leave above 10 of them to tell the tale [3] and we are having a few Tamworth boys come to look at us, it cheers them up a bit when they drop across one another. I dropped across young Kinson out of the Lays [4], I hardly knew him he looks well, he is coming down to spend the day with us today, you can tell his mother when you see her. Dear I think it will be about Aug for we shall get any leave, there are several going out of the Batt of course they have got good excuses it has to be family affairs or illness before they let them come and then they only come for 5 days and if I wait till Aug we shall get 7 days if all goes well which I hope so don't you dear so don't go and overwork yourself as it will be very disappointing for us both especially as we have been apart for such a long time so I want you to take great care of yourself as I am doing the same, never felt so better, keep on smiling (and in the Pink) and I don't think we need be afraid when we see one another again dear, what do you say. Dear I have had a letter from Inship and some fags, tell him I will write soon and Capt Jenkinson has left us gone to the base and I expect Caleb will be promoted again soon to Sergt Major, he is acting so now and Segt Layton will probably be over on leave soon for he has put in for a Pass for me and him an lying together and he has told me. Dear, I hope Hilda is better and tell the children they have got to behave themselves and pleased to hear your Dad touched a 10 to 1 [5], for they take some finding, I guess it was one of his olduns out of the bits. Dear I think this will be all this time for I am just going to have a bath should you like the job (what oh) [6] hoping to hear from you soon and roll on Aug. From your ever loving and dearest husband Syd X Fan XXXXXXXXXX and a few for the children XXXXXXXXXX.

P.S. Remember me to Dad and Nell hoping they are going on alright, from Syd XX.

P.S. Pleased with the currants, could not help but smile when I opened parcel and saw them.

Goodnight and God Bless you all XX.

Notes

1. Fan has sent Syd some sort of spirits through the post. This was officially banned, but Syd seems to have received his bottle OK.

2. The Market Place at Ypres, 1915. See page 38.

3. Men taken prisoner were killed on both sides, without doubt, but the majority were captured and sent to POW camps. Sidney Rogerson's excellent book 'Twelve Days On The Somme' gives an account of a group of soldiers who were trapped for two days in waterlogged trenches who "Insisted on sharing their infrequent mugs of tea with a wounded German. 'Here's a drop of tea for Fritz' the men would say, as they propped up the captive and fed him as a nurse would feed a patient."

4. Syd means The Leys, an area of Tamworth.

5. Fan's Dad has had a win on the horses.

6. Company Commanders were responsible for seeing that the men took a bath as often as possible. Of course, it was unlikely to be in a bath-tub! Anything available that could hold water would be used. This image shows men of the 1/6th South Staffords in

Visé Paris n° 42   42   GUERRE 1914-1916. — Entrée d'Ypres. — Entrance to Ypres. — LL.

Visé Paris n° 41   41   GUERRE 1914-1916. — Ypres en ruines. — Ruins of Ypres. — LL.

Visé Paris n° 504   504   GUERRE 1914-1916. — Ypres. — La Rue au Beurre. — Butter street. — LL.

Postcards showing the devastation of Ypres. Note that in card 3 the lines can be clearly seen.

Flanders, 1915 taking a bath in a wooden cart lined with a hay-rick cover. Water had apparently been heated in biscuit tins on a fire outside the barn.

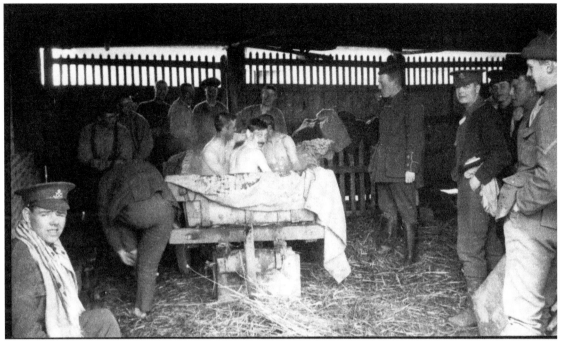

Flanders, 1915. Men of the 1/6th South Staffordshire Regiment taking a bath. At the same time as the men were bathing, their clothes might be put into a Foden Disinfector, a fumigating machine that would kill lice and their eggs so that clothes could be laundered and given out again. Strangely, some men reported feeling more uncomfortable when clean and in stiff new uniforms than when in their old lice-ridden clothing. Another way of delousing clothing in winter weather was to hang a shirt up to freeze, which would in turn kill any insect inhabitants. Sydney Rogerson recalls the humour that was generated even by lice infestation. A soldier comments to his comrade: "I'm making a collection, Nobby. I've got all kinds now except one with pink eyes and revolving teeth." Image ©Staffordshire Regiment Museum.

12.7.15

My Dear Wife,

I take the pleasure of writing to you after our experiences of 6 days and nights in a wood, we had several gruelling times we had 4 bombardments with artillery, the first bombardments we have been in and we came out top dog each time and our Comp had no casualties so we are lucky again, it was a beautiful wood, I quite enjoyed myself till the last day I fell sick. Pains in the head I had to go under the Doctor but I'm going alright now we have to march a long way when we come out about 12 miles to the rest place and march at night to get in about 6 o'clock in the morning and I'm thinking about you when we are marching along the road but we all seem happy and merry, some singing and some cursing and swearing and we are having nice weather of course, we have had several small showers of rain nothing to shout about. I see they have had plenty in (Blighty) and Jim Broadhurst is seriously wounded and I hear there is hopes of him going on alright. Dear I received your letters and parcel alright and had a parcel from Nelly which I enjoy in the trenches, tell Nell how I enjoyed the loaf and butter for it came in handy. We were getting short as they could not get to us for two days as they were shelling us and thanking her very much. She asked me to tell you in the letter and remember me to dad, tell him I shall see him soon if all's well. I am putting in for a Pass for the first week in Aug did you see anything of sergt Layton when he was over. I told him to call and see you. I expect it made you feel a bit (mad) but it can't be helped we must have a little patience till Aug if the war aint over by then for I hope it is as I don't like the idea of coming over to come back here again. I want to come back and stop for I don't think it will last a great much longer for there was five Germans came and gave themselves up, we got some good information out of them they said they were fed up being forced to fight and so there was a lot more coming in to give themselves up. We fired on them and only hit one. We handled them pretty rough, it took us all our time to keep the bayonet out of them and they are going to have another go at Calais, hope they will have some luck now, we have got plenty of shells. Dearest I have just received a small parcel from Mr Walker, tell him if you see him any time. I will write soon. Dear you never say anything about those postcards I sent you, that's the place I spent Easter in, and remember me to your dad has he had another 10 to 1 again, tell him to put us 3d on the next. I have been looking at a Herald, what do you think about Shannon's factory girls sending us Woodbines [1] you ought to have been here when they were giving them out, the remarks what was passed, especially when they knew where they came from. Well dear I think this is all this time, hoping we shall see one another soon (what a day we shall have in August) I shall keep my head down and let you know as soon as I get my Pass it only takes 9 hours to come so keep smiling. From your ever loving and affectionate husband Syd X Fan XXXXXXXXXX.

Give my love to the children and kiss them all for me from Dad XXXXXX.

Shannon's Mill. Image ©
The Tamworth Herald.

Postcard showing female factory workers.

Notes

1. In 1904 John Shannon and Son of Walsall bought the Lichfield Street Mill, Tamworth. In 1915 Shannon's Factory girls were making British uniforms. There was something rather risqué about factory girls. The fact that they earnt their own money and were in most cases unmarried gave them a certain frisson.

19.7.15

My Dearest Wife

Just a few more lines in answer to your welcome letters and parcel which cheered me up and was mostly enjoyed and I wished you good health for I hope to find you all in the best of health when I come over, hoping it will be soon for my pass has gone up to Headquarters and am waiting patiently every day for the date which I am coming as I will let you know soon as it comes through as I know you are anxiously waiting as well for it seems such a long while since we saw one another it's really too long to be apart, what do you say dear but never mind let me get over this lot, I will see we don't part again if we live to be 100 its alright in Blighty soldiering, its alright out here but not for married men. I hope I do come over soon I will tell them the tale especially if I have a pint or two thats all dear. Sergt Layton arrived back alright he said you all looked well and about the same, very pleased to hear it dear. I feel very sorry about Lucy, Toms oldest, hoping she is not going the wrong way for I could say a good deal in the matter for its nothing to do with me, I could not alter

---

things if I did hoping to hear better news about her when you write again for I was rather surprised as well, Dear I should like to bring the children something but we are not allowed they inspect them all before they get on the boat, try and tell them the tale or something, and I hope I shall be lucky to bring myself for we are still out of the trenches having a good time expecting to be going in again soon and expecting a big smash up as well but we are prepared, we are expecting it on the 15th, they had a try but it did not come off, wish they would have a good smash up it would perhaps have a great deal towards the end of the war for there are thousands of troops out here only waiting for the word to go and everything seems quiet just as present and we are having plenty of sport while we are out. I was in a cricket match, we finished it on Sunday the sergts playing the officers we beat them it was for 5 Francs a side but we didn't get it, I expect we shall when the war is over. Dear what sort of weather have you been having, we have had a nice drop of rain for 2 days very nearly washed us out and its terribly hot again, well I have not a great lot to tell you this time. Caleb and Jack are going on alright and the remainder of the Company and thanks for the tomatoes [1] I enjoyed a treat on Sunday morning with some ham my old favourite Sunday morning feed. Dear remember me to Dad and Nell and also your dad hoping to see them soon I think. That's all this time from a very true husband Syd X Fan XXXXX.

Give my love to the children. Pleased to hear they are going on alright and kiss them for me XXXXX and thanks for Arthurs letter which I am returning. Goodnight and God Bless you XXXXX

P.S. (Remember me to the chickens.)

Notes

1. This illustrates nicely the speed of the postal service. Fan is able to parcel up fresh tomatoes from her garden in Tamworth, and there is a good chance that they arrived with Syd the next day. Regular post was key to keeping up the troop's morale, and large sorting offices sprang up all over the country to deal with the huge tide of post coming in and out of the UK. There is a Post Office Lane in Rugeley where a WW1 sorting office was situated. In London, the largest wooden building ever constructed at that point sprang up specifically to sort and forward military mail.

29.7.15

My Dear Wife,

Just a few lines in answer to your loving letter I received on the 24th inst, pleased to hear you are all going on alright as it leaves me the same at present also in the pink, saving what a gruelling time we have had in the trenches with the whizz bangs, they knocked about 100 yards of our trenches down and there was no one hurt so we had to work all right to put them up and they tried to knock them down the next day but we was one too many for them, our artillery bringing all their trenches to the ground and we lost 2 killed and 20 injured, there was one chap from my company killed, really his own fault would not do as he was told and we have been in a very hot spot on the right of Hill 60 what there is left of it and now we have come out again, we are in a very nice place not allowed out in the daytime in the open on account of the German aeroplanes seeing us, but we seen a fine bit of sport on Sunday night, our aircraft brought 2 Germans down, one of them set on fire and the other shot down, they lost 3 the same day and we are out for 6 days and then go back again (curse it). Dear, Caleb will be over on Monday next have you heard about him coming on leave, hope he will have a good time which I guess he will and hope I shall be able to tell you in my next letter the date when I shall be coming as I have seen my Pass as it is waiting to be dated for they would not let us come both together, I told them I didn't care as long as I could come some time, what do you say dear. I see Ben Ault has got back alright and safe. He says he had a good time, he said he never saw anything of you, he saw some of the children. Dear, I notice you are glad I have some sport, I have some sport every day still hunting but not so bad as used to be we get plenty of baths now. Dear I see there is nothing much at Tamworth at Aug what I have seen in the Herald but I hope you enjoy yourself and have nice weather. I should like to send you the price of a drink only I have not drawn no money for a month we have no use for it where we are we get plenty of everything barring beer I couldn't touch a drop. Dear, but wait till I come over we will have a drink together and a good one, trusting in the Lord to keep me in his care till I come over on Pass, as I have not studied religion before but it's made me think some times since I have been out here. Dear we are still having some nice weather again and we have got Capt Jenkinson with us he has been from us for about a month looking well and you might tell Mr Walker when you see him any time, I will probably write in due course if I have time, tell him I am going on alright and hope to see him soon, hoping they are enjoying good health and remember me to Dad. Pleased to hear they are going on alright and also your dad, hoping he is still having his luck in and remember me to Bert Read should like to drop across him as young George came out here yet I should like you to let me know what Regt he is in and then I could enquire where they are if I should get in close quarters to them. Dear I think this is all this time, hoping you will see Caleb when he comes over and he will tell you more, I shall come directly he comes back. Give my love to the children and all enquiring friends, hoping to see them soon. From your ever loving husband Syd X Fan.

XXXXX For the children XXXXX and now one for you dear X Goodnight and God Bless you all.

Syd.

5.8.15 Belgium.

My dear love,

In answer to your loving letters I received on (Weds). Pleased to hear you are all going on alright as it leaves me the same at present and still working hard and expecting a rest when we come out of the trenches this time for we have been in for 18 days close to [1] We are getting very weak what with killed and wounded and sick. I had 60 men in my Platoon once and now I have only got about 28, they sent us some men from the base but they have gone sick, there is a lot of sickness breaking out in our lot I think it's the water that's lots to do with it but we have to boil it before we drink it [2], some don't stop to boil it, they drink it almost a purpose and there is a terrible lot of flies about [3] as well but I am very careful and lucky with my meals and I take occasionally beechams every week I don't want to be sick out here on this job. I want to keep my health and strength up (you know trust me). Dear Fan I thought I should have been able to let you know when I were coming over but I was to have come on the 11th and Caleb on the 4th but all the Passes were stopped till further notice (hard lines) for we were expecting something on the 4th August and had to be prepared but there was nothing came off only on our left there was a battle, I expect you saw it in the paper where they spurted burning liquid on them [4] (the dogs), they took us by surprise but they did not have it all their own road at the finish they rushed up almost 12 deep and they were simply mown down and drove back. I saw the accounts in the paper this morning, they don't tell you all so you can see the reason I could not let you know as it was hard lines on Caleb, he had got his passes signed and arranging to come and everything and got so much money from the Headquarters, he was wild. I expect we shall be hearing something about our Passes this next week when we are out of the trenches hoping to let you know as soon as we hear any tidings for everything seems pretty quiet at present only at night time it's like being in L [5]. Whizz bangs [6] all night right and left, for the few lads I have got it takes me all my time to keep them from going over the parapet, they aint alf out for blood some of them.

Dearest I wished you sent me a parcel it would have just have come in handy where we are, but still we have gone on alright together, I have had plenty of cake with the others, sharing up the parcels they have sent them, there is only me and three corporals together in our little dug out, well furnished, we have got the Bombs in now get no money, no rent, we make our own amusement with telling funny stories nothing rude. Dear Fan I have got lots of funny stories to tell you when I come but I shall have to tell you some in French hoping it will be soon what do you say (bow wow) and we are having nice growing weather, plenty of sunshine and rain. Dearest I think this will be all this time don't be put out about me unable to let you know about coming for I am almost sure to come this month so Cheer oh and keep smiling and give my love to the children and also remember me to Dad and Nell and all enquiring friends in old Tam, they tell me the town hall is still there. I must draw to a close, from your ever loving

husband Syd X Fan. XXXXXXXXXXXXXX
For the kiddies XXXXXX. And God Bless you all from Dad XXXXXX and another
one for you dear X. Goodnight.

Notes

1. Men were only officially meant to spend a maximum of five days in the trenches. As you can see, this was the ideal but rarely the norm.

2. One of the major issues with drinking water in the trenches was down to the way it was transported. More often than not, empty petrol cans were simply refilled with drinking water (they should have been burnt out first). Drinking water laced with petrol will make you extremely nauseous and will often cause vomiting. If enough is ingested over a long enough period symptoms get very nasty and include breathing difficulties, vision loss, bloody stools, dizziness, headaches and loss of alertness. Syd sometimes complains of headaches, it may well be being caused by petrol in the water. As you can imagine, it also made everything taste foul, so foul that men had to be restrained from simply scooping up the slimy water from the trench floor and boiling that up for tea.

3. The earth that made up the walls of the trench, and the soil of No Man's Land would have been a mixture of earth, liquefying human and horse flesh, blood, vomit, excrement and urine. If a man suffered a direct hit from a shell, he could be effectively vaporised, scattering the earth with his remains. In addition, men were meant to relieve themselves in ideal circumstances in a latrine pit dug in a spur off the main trench, or often simply into a bucket that would then be carried away to the latrine, or behind the lines to a central midden. In reality, men used the buckets, or squatted on the ground to defecate and then either slung the bucket's contents over the top into No Man's Land or flicked the excrement over on the small entrenching spades they used to cut and repair the trenches. This, in a situation where the trench was under fire or under scrutiny from snipers is quite understandable. However, when mortars then hit No Man's Land, they would scatter the mixture of ordure and other fetid material back into the trench. No wonder there were flies about.

4. Syd is referring here to the German use of flame-throwers. The flame-thrower was a terrifying weapon used by the Germans against the British in 1915, and by the French and British after this date when they developed their own. The Germans called them either Flammenwerfers (hand-held portable versions) or Grossflammenwerfers (that needed wheeled transportation). Flame-throwers shoot out burning fuel and they could spurt flame for 36 metres. Flame-thrower operators had a short life expectancy as they were loathed and targeted by the Infantry. Often, the equipment would also explode.

5. L is short for Hell.

6. Whizz Bags were a kind of shell that made a whizzing sound when coming over and a bang when detonated.

Postcard showing French Officers and American Infantry using flamethrowers.

14.8.15

Flanders.

My dearest wife,
In answer to your loving letter I received (Thurs) pleased to hear you are all going on alright and also the children as it leaves me the same at present after my rough journey in the trenches, wishing it was the last time and it was all over so we could be together once again for every week seems a month to me, I don't know how it is with you I expect the same love, and sorry you were disappointed me not coming over and we have not heard anything yet about coming, we have made enquiries but without avail but they tell us there will be a surprise for us when we have been in the trenches once again, hoping it will be a Great Surprise as I am waiting for a (kiss and a squeeze, not half). Dear we have had a concert and the General has presented the DCMS to those three chaps Roland Hill and co. Very nice medals something to be proud of too, we had a bit of a booze up on the strength of them. I expect you will see all about them in the herald. I guess it was on Friday. Dear Fan, are you going to the sports next Sat I saw the advert in the paper. I should love to be over, it doesn't seem long since we saw the aeroplanes go over does it. Dear I received the parcel alright whilst in the trench which I enjoyed immensely especially the drop of Dew Drop for it kept my nerves up whilst we were expecting a scrap from Fritz when they started shelling but they were soon quietened down when our guns started. I got a bit of a rough and tumble, got buried twice with sandbags where the shells dropped close to our trench but held on the bottle alright, gave a wounded a little drop and we lost 6 killed out of our Comp this time and a few wounded, none from Tam so I can shake

hands with myself once again. Dear, Caleb has had a postcard from Eva asking him to go over to Northampton when he comes, what a nerve he will have some time to spend in 3 days if he has the luck to come, I should think it ought to be the other road about what do you think. Dear Fan, thank Arthur very much for the pocket book for it was just what I was going to ask you to send me for I am writing in it already, hoping he still is keeping a good boy till I come home for I shall bring him a souvenir what Fritz has sent me, what we call the Germans now and something else besides for they are fed up as well as us they threw bits of paper over to us in a bacca box with writing on so you can tell how close we are for I am not allowed to tell what was on the paper, nothing important. [1] Well dear, I think this is all this time, sorry I can't tell you when I am coming, hope I shall do soon, remember me to Dad and Nell, and also your Dad and give my love to the Children, and kiss them for me, remember me to all enquiring friends.

From your ever loving and fondest love and a kiss from Syd X Fan XXXXXXXXXXXX

For the children XXXXX and God Bless them. From Dad.

Goodnight all.

Notes

1. In the autobiographical 'Goodbye to All That' by Robert Graves, the author talks about just this situation occurring. He recalls a time when the Germans started to throw over tins that contained brief written messages. These notes contained nothing that could be construed as traitorous, but mainly little jokes. I find the fact that they were doing this heartbreakingly poignant.

20.8.15

Belgium

My Dear (lonesome) wife,

My kind regards to your loving letter I received on (Thurs). Pleased to hear you are going on alright as it leaves me the same at present and what about Caleb coming and taking you by surprise, hoping he has had a good time wish it was me as well, for I don't think it will be long before I get my leave as there is three batches coming as soon as we get out of the trenches, hoping it will be soon. I gave him some P. Cards [1] to give you, I expect he will tell you all the news for he had not much time to catch the train for it was short notice so don't be surprised to see me walking in some fine morning unawares and finding you all in bed and bringing you a cup of tea upstairs (I am almost forgot how) if I don't feel shy and you say they are going to take a bit off the top of the old house at last I hope they do and make a good job of it as we shall take some shifting if I come back again safe and what about when I come over and find you are with Mrs Reade it will be hard lines again (shall I have to go to Priscilla's) [2] well I think I can shave in-between somehow as I can't find you lodgings very well out here just where we are at present as there are no houses with a top on at all and I saw two women and three children have a narrow escape the other day whilst in charge of 20 men in a village which was being shelled we had just got by there came a shell straight through the roof and cleared the lot, the women had just come out about five minutes before. Of course that's nothing to some of the places we see as we go along out here and I should like to drop across George out here, I can't be very far from him if he has been in the trenches, if I only knew what Regt he was in I could find him and talk to him on the phone as I have got his number. Dear you won't half be in it for company directly when Lucy gets at Tam, tell them I think I shall get a job at Hall End [3] when I get back (I don't think). Dear I have not received the parcel yet, hoping that drink will if the parcel don't as it is very useful in the nights, for it gets very cold now for I want something to warm it (bow wow) [4] and I see you are having some rough weather different to us, its grand weather out here good job for us it is. I will bring you some hot weather when I come over and tell Arthur to take care of himself does he go out with no hat on like he used to do. Jack Butler has gone to do a bit of farm work for the Staff mowing and etc better than being in the trenches. I wish I could get a soft job, no such luck [5], they are sending a lot down to Rouen for a rest when we get out this time I don't know whether I am going yet or not, I shall tell them to send me to Blighty for my rest, what do you say. Well dear, I think this will be all this time hope we shall see one another soon, from your loving husband Syd X Fan XXX

Love to the children and kisses XXXXXX and God Bless them.

Goodnight and God Bless you all, Syd X.

Notes

1. As soon as Allied forces arrived in France and Belgium the locals began to realise that the enterprising could make money from all of these men who had regular pay (if they decided to draw it) but very little to spend it on. A roaring trade started in embroidered postcards (Syd calls them p cards or P.C.s). They would be embroidered by locals with either floral garlands or military themed designs alongside a message such as 'Fond Thoughts from Over the Sea' and could be either put into an envelope and sent home to a wife, mother or girlfriend or couriered home by a fellow soldier on leave. These postcards have become very collectable. Gifts could also be made from spent bullet casings or shell casings. Sometimes an ordinary soldier would spend time bending and manipulating the metal into a gift such as a matchbox cover, a toy tank, an ashtray or a vase, but more often the men of the Royal Engineering Corps would use the tools that they had easily to hand to make items that they would sell

A bullet that has been made into a portable cross. Artefact from the collection of the Staffordshire Regiment Museum.

on. This little bullet has been fashioned into a portable cross that could stand on a mantelpiece. These sorts of gifts are known now as 'trench art' and are again very collectable.

2. It seems very likely that Pricilla's was a local brothel.

3. This is probably Morris and Shaw Colliery at Hall End – A mine that in the period, like so many, had a reputation for poor safety.

4. Syd is alluding to needing his wife to 'warm him up'.

5. If a soldier is ordered to do a job they have to do it. That job might cover anything from filing papers to operating as an Officer's batman or servant. Syd refers here to a comrade being given a job mowing hay and wishes he could join him as jobs out of the front line were less dangerous and provided better rations. In WW1 there were whole Battalions of soldiers doing manual work, one such Battalion was known as the Pioneers. Duties would involve manual labour including road building and repair or even forestry work and logging. There's no favouritism being shown here, soldiers were busy at a whole range of jobs all the time.

29.8.15

Chateau Belgie

My darling wife,

A few lines in hand to your welcome letter I received on Sat night, I had just returned from a hot quarter with a party of 50 men and in a very bad temper for some of them struck a match and gave our position away and they didn't half pepper us, a most serious thing, but I could not find the right man who did it or I would have had him shot there and there but as luck had it we only had one wounded but I made my position alright but it is not settled yet. I had to make a report so I don't know how it will end [1] but when I got your letter it put all the trouble to one side for it didn't half cheer me up and I had an issue of rum so you can see how we spend (Sat) nights out here for I don't want to have many more (Sat) nights like it I can tell you but never mind we shall have to make up for it when it's all over for I must think myself a lucky chap as its better to be born lucky than rich they say and its true for the dangerous position we are in. Well dear, Caleb has arrived back alright told me what a beano you had together at Fazeley, very pleased to hear it wish I had been there we should have had a better one together (not half) and then we shall have some sport over the (Station Fields) [2] I bet you don't half feel mad sometimes (for I do) especially when some of the chaps come home from leave especially the married men. Well dear I have seen the Capt today Sun about my Pass he told me he should let me come on or about the 20th of Sept if I didn't mind till then as there are some particular cases and also giving some of the Privates a chance and they will be extending the leave to 10 or 12 days and more men coming at a time. I see Pte Talbot is coming on the 10th, perhaps you will see him for he is fatter than ever he was. Dear we are having nice weather, glad you are and we are in a nice Chateau better than the dug outs, don't fancy ourselves. Plenty of shells dropping round us we can go boating or fishing[3], there is a nice pond close to but I am trying to fish for my ticket but nothing doing and we have had a Church Parade this morning while they were burying 2 comrades at the same time. Plenty of cemeteries about here and I have had my name mentioned at Headquarters, the hard work which has been done whilst being in charge, hoping I get through alright. Well dear, I think this is all this time will soon fly. Remember me to Brash and family and your Dad and Nell. From your ever loving husband Syd X Fan. XXXXX. Give my love to the children, I expect they are awaiting anxiously to see me XXXXX.

P.S. I received the parcel but it had a severe shaking, but I gave the bottle a good shaking but when you send some more tomatoes send the tins for they get broke and some foot power, don't send any sort of clothing for I get plenty, I have got a brand new suit, don't half look smart. Have you seen Mr Walker, I wrote to him last week. Goodnight and God Bless you all.

Syd XXXXX.

Notes

1. It may sound harsh to us - threatening to shoot the man who struck a match and showed a light, but Syd had just spent a hellish night being bombarded with bullets and shells as the Germans tried to wipe him and his comrades out. That one act could have cost 50 men their lives.

2. Caleb has been to visit Syd's wife and has spent Whitsun with them. Syd is here alluding to a famous spot for lovers 'Station Fields'. It is still an area of open fields now used as a static home and caravan site.

Men of the 6th South Staffords fishing behind the lines. Image © Staffordshire Regiment Museum.

The Battle of Loos

Syd's battalion, the 1/6th North Staffords were heavily involved in the fighting at the Battle of Loos in 1915, and at Gommecourt on the northern flank of the Battle of the Somme. The following is a brief outline of the main points of the battle, but a much more evocative description is given in Caleb's letter to his brother Syd, reproduced below and kept by the family for decades.

In the year 1915, 285,107 men died on the Western Front. Almost a fifth of those men died at the Battle of Loos. The Battle of Loos was the largest British offensive of 1915 on the Western Front and the first time the British used poison gas. The battle's objective was for the French and British to break through the German lines around Artois and Champagne as things were at a stalemate. The Allies were not successful and the British, French and German casualty rate was very high.

Before the battle, tunnels had been dug under the German lines and filled with extraordinary amounts of high explosive. At the commencement of the offensive they were detonated. The British were low on ammunition from the start, and much of the 140 tonnes of chlorine gas released by our forces blew back and killed many of our own.

The battle began on 25th September. The German barbed wire had not been cut in advance and as the British advanced towards the Germans they were cut down by machine gun fire. Despite this the British managed to break through and capture the town of Loos. On 3rd October the Germans attacked and recaptured the Hohenzollern Redoubt. On 8th October, the Germans again attempted to recapture much of the lost ground but failed. On the 13th October the British launched a final attack which also failed, possibly due to a lack of Mills Bombs.
British casualties in the Battle of Loos came to 59,247

Syd has been wounded...

Letter dated some time after 13th October 1915

Crept about 200 yards on my stomach into a safe place till the stretcher bearers could get to me expecting every minute was my last. As I was being carried away they were pinging at as but Oh when I knew I was in a safe place I prayed and thanked the Lord above twice, I could see him on my right and you and the children on my left. But dear, don't put yourself about I am very comfortable and being well looked after. I only wished they had have put me a bit closer to home so you could come and see me but never mind you will know I am in a safe place and in Old England again it's a very nice place where I am about 200 in the same ward and they are all strangers to me, I don't know any of them it's about 14 miles from Plymouth on the sea coast. I shall be able to tell you more about it next letter.[1] I arrived here on Sat night at 6. I started from a place called Bethune in France in a hospital train, it took us 26 hours to get to Le Havre. I was in a bed nicely fitted up but in awful pain on my back could not move and then I got to No.2 General Hospital and got my wound dressed before going on the Hospital Ship and then we moved on to the ship into beds all fitted up to date, Doctors coming to see all the while, and nurses galore and then I landed at Southampton and we had to stop in the harbour all night till Sat morning and then put into a hospital train here, it took us 10 hours to get to the Hospital so you can see I had a bit of knocking about. Well Dear, what is putting me about I can't hear no tidings of Caleb and Jack, has Liza heard anything, do let me know for I think all the Tamworth lads got wounded.

Notes

1. At the beginning of the war soldiers when wounded could be sent to hospitals and nursing homes close to their home towns to recuperate. This was soon changed however as the sight of so many appallingly maimed and wounded men was effecting the morale of the country. Soldiers were now sent to large nursing homes, often commandeered large country houses, to recuperate. Being away from home also lessened the temptation to go AWOL.

BETHUNE. — *Vue générale prise du Beffroi.* — *LL.* Visé Paris n° 88

The bustling city of Bethune before the war.

The following letter was sent to Syd by his brother Caleb. It is a grim account of the Battle of Loos, a battle all three brothers fought in.

30/10/1915

Dear Brother, I was very pleased to hear from you and that you are going on alright. Also hoping that you will soon be able to get about again, I am enjoying the very best of health. I expect you are anxious to know how we are going on what was left of us. I like yourself on 18.10.15 experienced a terrible time I did not see you go over the parapet. As soon as my Platoon got over I had Cpl Fradley shot dead. The next I saw was Pte March badly bleeding. He asked me not to leave him, I called for the stretcher bearers, then I had to leave him. The next I saw was Captain Jenkinson shot through the leg, he fell and the stretcher bearers came to him and they were also shot down. One was killed, Pte Neville of my Platoon, 3 was wounded. The next I saw was L/Sgt Platts and Henney shot and several more, I then advanced into the first line trench I found about all the officers had been shot. I got my men together then rushed into the second line trench without losing a man of my platoon on the second rush. I think there was a great mistake in rushing the first line in short rushes, we lost a lot of men by doing so, a rush straight across would have been a success. We were all exposed to fire, I dropped myself into a shell hole. I stopped in the first trench about ten minutes, I told the men to prepare to advance into the next line of trench about two hundred yards away without halting, and they did. I was very pleased to know all got across without a man getting hit. I then got an order from Colonel Radcliffe to hold this trench, so this stopped us from advancing any further. Here I found us mixed up with all sorts of Regiments South and North Staffords, Lincolns and Leicesters, we were having it very hot with bombs, but we gave them more than they gave us. It was a fine bit of work to see young Schofield of my Platoon running the Germans up the communication trench with bombs. I never expected him to come back, but he did in an awful sweat, he had used all his bombs. Things quietened down a bit then I walked along the trench. I witnessed a terrible sight of killed and wounded and no stretcher bearers to be found. Men was in awful pain. I dressed a lot of their wounds and then sent them out of the trench. Them that could not walk had to lie in the trench in awful pain for twelve – eighteen hours or more. I was enquiring for you and Jack for some time before I could hear anything. I heard you had been wounded and gone out, but not serious. Next I saw in the trench was Pte Bott, he was dying from a very bad wound. Next I met Sergt Major Gee, he was alright but like myself had enough. I then came across pte Harris lying dead with three other men I did not know. Next I met L/Cpl Mallet, he had been over the top and fetched in two wounded. I begged of him not to go over again, he would not be persuaded by me, he went did not go far before he was hit never to rise again, it was the case of several men throwing their lives away trying to save the wounded, but it was murder to go. Next I was pleased to meet Jack, he was alright as if nothing had happened, although he was very lucky, he took with him when he made the charge three loaves of bread and a tin of butter (he did not mean starving) in a sandbag, when he took the bread out he found three bullets had passed through the bread so you see he was lucky, but I think every one of us are lucky to be alive. Next I met Olner and Ault, they were alright. By this time it was getting dark and I thought it was a good opportunity to get in what wounded we could, first we got in the Captain (Talbot helped) he lay in the open for several hours, for it would have been certain death to have gone out to him. After a struggle we got him in, it was a case of being cruel to be kind. As he lay on the fire step he asked for a doctor. We could not do anything for there was not an ambulance man to be found. We made him as comfortable as we could. I could see he had been hit again for he had an awful wound in the stomach. I watched over him, I could see he could not last long. He lasted about an hour, then we put him into a small disused trench close by. We covered him over, it was an awful night, foggy and damp. The enemy tried a counter attack but were repulsed. At daybreak they continued to shell us. Then I found out Sergt L Hayward had been hit by a shell but did not see him. All day long we stuck to the trench expecting counter attacks, but it was an artillery duel all day long. About 4 o'clock we had news that we were going to be relieved at 9 o'clock but unfortunately did not get relieved until seven the next morning by the guards. I shall never forget that Saturday morning when we left the trenches, the spectacle presented was that of a true battlefield. In the tangle of torn barbed wire were to be seen the scattered bodies of the slain, many of them being held up in a more or less upright position. This is where I saw the last of the Captain I had an unpleasant job to search him. I had to take everything from him and make a list of things he had on him. I should have liked some of his things for a remembrance of him but the only thing I had was his collar badges and stars which I hope to keep in remembrance of him. Next we got the order to file out. I had to get to the rear and see every man what was left of us was out of the trench and the Guards took our duties. I should say I was the last man of the Company to see the captain. I had a good look at him before leaving. On we marched through the communication trenches. When we arrived at the end we were surprised to find those tram buses awaiting for us, they took us to a place the other side of Vermelles, halted and had breakfast in a farmyard, here we were visited by the General and the Prince of Wales he said he was proud of us. We had all done what was expected of us. We next went on to [here Caleb has left a gap, in effect censoring his own letter] about the same billets we had left. A few days there then we went on to a place seven miles to [censored] Stayed there seven days then came back to [censored] where we are at the time of writing. Have much the same duties as we have always been having. We have not been in the trench again, there is no sign of us going just yet, but we have a carrying party of about 120 each battalion, find it plenty for a week. Notts and Derbys last week it is our battalion this week. I may tell you I have been made Coy2. M. Srgt of A. Company Sergt Major Brindley was amongst the killed and Sergt Major Tuby wounded. Our battalion lost heavily. I was the only Sergt that came out without a scratch. In fact all the officers and NCOs suffered a lot, there were only three officers with the Colonel and Adjutant came out of it. Sergt Copeland, Sergt Harris, Sergt Cutler, Sergt Stone was killed and others, yourself, Platts, Austin, Kenny, Hammond, Watts, Sherley, Cpl Burrows, Clements, Littleford, Cronise (wounded). I cannot remember them all. Smasher Smith has died of his wounds also Mason. You will be surprised when you see the list of the lot. We had a roll call next morning, I shall never forget it. The strength were A. Company 90, B. 92, C. 112, D. 114. We have had a draft of officers and NCOs and men from Rouen of about two hundred. Heaths son as used to be inspector of Tamworth is an Officer in C Company. I am living at a good place myself and Coy Sergt Major Oldham. Have got a bed to lay in, the first since we have been out, got a servant, so you can guess we are alright. I have been asked by the undermentioned names who have always been asking about if I had heard from you, all the Tamworth men, Sergt Olner, Summers (just been on leave) also L/Cpl Allsop and L.Stretton, Ault, Lt/Cpl Charlesworth, Cpl Clements and sergt B Norton is reported killed of Burton. He has not been heard of. Also L. Mitchell was wounded. I think I have said all this time, hoping to hear from you good news of you improving. I hope by the time you are better it will be over but I doubt it. I expect you have received your letters. I kept them back until I heard from you. Also I took possession of your kit, there was nothing in it of any value, but your razor and I kept that. I will close now.

Stretcher bearers of the 2nd North Staffords – 1915. Image © Staffordshire Regiment Museum.

Dr. Brother,

I was very pleased to hear from you and that you are going on alright. also hoping that you will soon be able to get about again I am enjoying the very best of health. I expect you are anxious to know how we are going on. what was left of us. I like yourself on 18th 1915. esperienced a torreable time i did not see you as over the parapet. As soon as my platoon got over i had. Cpl. Bradley shot dead. the next i saw was Pte. Marsh. badly bleeding. he asked me not to leave him i called for stretcher bearers. then I had to leave him. the next i saw was Captain Jackson. shot. through the leg. he fell. & the stretcher bearers come to him. and they were also shot down one was killed Pte. Neville of my platoon. there was wounded. the next i saw was Sergt. Platts. & Kenney. shot. and several more. i then advanced into the first line trench. i found about all the officers had been shot. i got my men together then rushed into the second line trench. without loosing a man of my platoon on the second rush, I think there was a great mistake in rushing the first line in short rushes. we lost a lot of men by doing so. a rush strenght across would have (been) a success. we were all exposed to fire. i droped myself in a shell hole. I stoped in the first trench about ten minutes. i told the men to prepair to advance in to the next line of trench. about two hundred yds away. without aulting. and they did. i was very pleased to know all got across without a

The extraordinary letter of Sergeant Caleb Norton of C Company, 1/6th North Staffords, sent to his brother Syd after the conclusion of the Battle of Loos. Document from the collection of the Staffordshire Regiment Museum.

(In France) 23.2.16

To Sergt S Norton

Dear friend,
Just a few lines to let you know that I have received your welcome letter which you write on the 11.1.16 Sorry to hear that you are going through it a bit as me and all the boys are enjoying good heath except Talbot and he has had a touch of rheumatism and lost a stone or two but he is picking up a bit now. Well Syd J. Charlesworth is going on alright and I don't know if you know but he is a Lance sergt and you talk about NCOs well we get a --- in our platoon and that is [censored] as I believe he is after another stripe and he comes from the same place as the sergt major who used to be in D.Coy and he is no good to the men. Well Sergt I suppose you will be surprised to know we have been to Egypt and stopped out there for about a month and then came back after they had nearly clambed[1] us to death three biscuits for one man and a tin of bully beef for four.
Well Sergt there are still some of the boys left in the Platoon, Kegy, Scruby, Tommo, Hunter, Stanhouse and Smiler all enjoying good health excepting Cpl Burrows who has not been up to the mark lately. Well Sergt it has been about three months since we were in the trenches and as far as I can tell you we are going in again on Saturday towards Arras so I suppose we shall have a hot time. Well Sergt I think I have said all this time hoping you and your brother will soon get well again.
From your sincerely,
G O. Lees
P.S. All the boys and Friends wish to be remembered to you and hope you will go on alright.

Notes
1. Starved.

I wore a Tunic
I wore a tunic, a lousy khaki tunic,
And you wore your civvy clothes.
We fought and bled at Loos,
While you were home on the booze,
The booze that no one here knows.
Oh you were with the wenches,
While we were in the trenches,
Facing an angry foe.
Oh you were a-slacking,
While we were attacking,
The Jerry on the Menin Road.

We have no more letters from Syd, but what he and his brother left us are as vivid a set of eye witness accounts as I have ever read. Syd lived into his 90s and died in the county he was born in.

The Letters of Sergeant James Stevenson of the 9th Battalion North Staffordshire Regiment

In 1911 James Stevenson was living at 110 Lower Spring Road, Longton. The household at 110 Lower Spring Road was a crowded one containing James and Eliza who were both 28. They had been married for six years and were living with Eliza's family. At this time James is listed as a China Cup Turner. They live with their daughter Ada who is four, George Bailey, James' father-in-law (51) who is a coal miner, Arthur Bailey, James' brother-in-law (21) who is a colliery wagoner, Ada (19), Nellie (17) and Florence Bailey (14) who are all sisters-in-law and work as Potter's Cup Casters or Handlers, and finally James Bailey (7) who is Eliza's little brother. James is listed as the Head of the Household, quite a responsibility for a young man of 28.

By 1914 things had moved on and James and Eliza Stevenson ran a shop on Normacott Road in Longton, Stoke-on-Trent called Uncle Tom's Cabin, that combined the selling of general groceries with a small 'off licence' or bar.

James is a kind, gentle and poetic man who proves himself to be a courageous soldier. Unlike Sergeant Norton, Sergeant Stevenson's letters are less factual and more emotional. They are outpourings of love for his family, sent from a man who has been in the thick of the fighting for three years. He is lonely and exhausted but full of hope.

Home of the Stevenson family, 154 Normacott Road, Longton, Stoke-on-Trent. This image is part of The Lovatt Collection: Copyright Stoke-on-Trent City Archives. Image reference SD 1253-1-0304. This image was taken in the 1950s. It shows Uncle Tom's Cabin (with shuttered windows) on the left.

Hush, here comes a Whizz-bang

Hush, here comes a Whizz-bang.
Hush, here comes a Whizz-bang.
Now you soldiermen get down those stairs,
Down in your dug-outs and say your prayers.
Hush, here comes a Whizz-bang,
And it's making right for you.
And you'll see all the wonders of No-Man's-Land,
If a Whizz-bang, hits you.

James Stevenson. Sketch by Carl Knibb.

Sunday 6pm 6/5/17

Dear daughter

With fondest love I now take the pleasure to answer your ever welcome letter which I received today dated April 25th. I received one from Mamma too, shall reply to that in the morning, I am very pleased to see that you have improved in health and your little brothers too, but I am awfully sorry to see that "Mamma" does not enjoy better health yet, she must feel miserable with those terrible rheumatic pains day after day, and the worry of the shop and children too. I am pleased to say that I am quite well myself and safe for the present, I also see you got the 5/- alright. I shall send you more presently, you make me smile when I see the games of young "Des" I feel so content now about him, now that he has got back home again "Mamma" will soon pull him together again. One thing I noticed particularly in your letter which pleased me very much was the vast improvement in your writing, Mamma tells me in her letter that Mr Tomlinson has come out to France I may have the pleasure of seeing him if so I will let you know. The weather is very hot out here now I hope you are getting it nice at home too so that you can all get out and try to benefit your health. Give my best wishes to "Grand-pa" and Aunt Ada and all at home, kiss all the other children for me and I will conclude with happiest thoughts of you all and sweetest love and affectionate remembrance.
From your ever loving "Dad" XXXXXXXXXX For all the children XXXXXXXXXX For "Mamma"

Letter fragment

Friday 11am 6/7/17

"Plucked off the Battlefield"
My dearest sweetheart and loving little children, with fond memories I now take the pleasure to drop you another word of love, in the best of health and still safe [several words obscured as paper is torn off here]. Or even what we have to put up with, I am in the open country on the battlefield miles and miles from anywhere, only a bleak wilderness, as I am writing this letter I am obliged to get under cover as 'Fritz' is shelling us all around, no peace anywhere, night or day, my darling sweetheart, you cannot possibly picture it, so therefore

Battlefields would be shorn of any distinguishing feature. Image shows a blasted oak, Ypres. ©Staffordshire Regiment Museum.

MY GOD, MY FATHER (4).
RENEW MY WILL FROM DAY TO DAY,
BLEND IT WITH THINE AND TAKE AWAY
ALL THAT NOW MAKES IT HARD TO SAY,
"THY WILL BE DONE."
BAMFORTH.(Copyright).

Bamforth song card.

In the field
Thursday 8pm 6/9/17

To My Bonnie Sweet Flowers
I am just like the Bee
Waiting to settle on
Your lips o'er the sea

My Darling wife
And sweet little ones. With faithful love I now take great pleasure to answer your beautiful loving letter that I have just received dated August 31st it is the first I have had for 4 days. I am sorry to see that you have been without a letter from me for over a week as I have wrote to you continuously day after day I missed for about 4 days not long ago which was quite necessary on account of me being held tight up the line through something I cannot state through my letters. That is the only time I slackened off writing so you should be getting them alright now, I see by your letters you have received 3 at once so you see I am telling you correct, now I am glad to see that all the children are still keeping well and perky. But I am sorry to see you are so poorly and downhearted I know you are tired of it my sweet love, but for my sake don't give way bear up to it now we have stood 3 years of it so do your best my sweetheart to battle through the rest, I can see how you love me and want me to come back to you all again I only wish I could to ease your weary hearts my darling, if you only knew how I yearn now to come to you all you would know how truly you all are loved, but I cannot the only hope I can see yet is my leave and that is heartily welcomed both by myself and you and my dear little ones, I am pleased to say I am still in the pink and safe yet, we are still up the line, hell I mean. Kiss my sweet little children for me I am very glad to hear that "Arthur's" wife is improving and hope she will continue. I know "J Lawton" quite well, I'm very sorry to hear of it but I'm not surprised to hear of anyone there'll be none left just now if it lasts much longer. I always used to say I was one of the unlucky ones in the world but, with thanks to God for the same and to you my darlings for your reverent prayers for me which I know are sent straight to him for my benefit because your heart holds a sacred love for me only as I have for you and he has heard you and knows both sides to be faithful and true to each other and our dear little children as we both promised through the bonds of marriage under his sacred name and I firmly believe that he has had his hand guiding me through my rugged course for the miraculous escapes I have had are too numerous to mention and the "hells" that I have passed through seemed utterly impossible for any man to live through but I am still kicking with good spirits and going through a hell each day and night because I know across the sea at some very near date I shall leave this behind me for a short time and sail merrily to "home sweet home" in dear old Blighty where dear fine loving hearts are aching and waiting to catch me and kiss me and take me

to their loving hearts and love me as I am yearning for the same "Oh" my dear ones, I cannot tell you how I love you and how much I want you, all of you, cheer up, my loved ones, I shall come some day. I shall meet you with a fine kiss as sweet as the lily, what a gift to me when I can just catch sight of your sweet face again on the station how I shall love you all God only knows, well my darlings I must conclude now and wish you all goodnight and God Bless you and keep you safe until we meet again with ever fondest love and faithful devotion to you all

From your affectionate and ever loving husband and Daddie XXXXXXXXXX for my dear children XXXXXXXXXX for my true loving wife.

Bamforth song card.

Letter fragment.

Sunday 10.30am 23/9/17
My dear loving children:
With sweetest and fondest love and thoughts of you all I take great pleasure to answer your beautiful letter that I received yesterday dated Sept 17 written by "Ada", very pleased to find that all of you are keeping so well and "Mamma" a little better as I am quite well myself and still safe, I am also very pleased to hear through "Mammas" letter that you have been raised to standard V, I see also that they have had a nice ceremony at the church on the occasion of the unveiling of a splendid "Role of honour", and my name is upon it, I suppose you would be present at the ceremony, I must try to see it when I come home on

In the Field
Sunday 10.30am 23/9/17
Dear wife and children-:
With fondest love and thoughts of you all I now take the pleasure to answer your ever welcome letter that I received yesterday dated Sept 18th very glad to find the children all keeping so well and you yourself improving again, I am quite well myself and still safe. I also hope I shall hear good news of "Dad" when I receive your next letter it seems as though he had a tight pinch of it, give my best wishes to him and all friends and kiss the children for me. I have sent our "Ada" a letter on, I am also sending on tomorrow a registered letter containing £2, for winter school coats and gloves for the children, the weather keeps very nice out here yet it begins to get very cold at night with the smell of winter in it, I hope you are successful in getting the 3 loads of coal that you state for the winter it will help you a good stretch through the cold weather, as I see they are going to limit the people to certain weights per week, I do hope they let you have it as you cannot do without a good fire with a family of little ones knocking about the kitchen in cold weather, we can put up with the cold but we must keep the little ones warm if at all possible so I hope you are successful then you will be alright for a good period anyway at the same time getting the weekly allowance from the coal wharf, well I must close now and wish you all good day and God bless you with the fondest and most affectionate love from your ever loving husband and "Dad"
XXXXXXXXXX For yourself with love from husband
XXXXXXXXXX For the children with love from "Dad."

Friday 3pm 28/9/17

Dear wife and children-:

With fondest love I now take great pleasure to answer your ever welcome letter that I received yesterday dated sept 23rd, very pleased to see that you and the children are all quite well and "Dad" improving, I am quite well myself and still safe, I am very sorry to hear of Mrs Edkin's death and hope I shall have the pleasure of meeting Mr Edkin at an early date on the occasion of my leave, please convey my deepest sympathy to him in his sad bereavement, give my best wishes to all at home and all friends and kiss the children for me, I hope you have received the registered letter alright that what you ask me about is the same, shall write again tomorrow so I'll close now with best love to you all

From your ever loving husband and "Dad"

XXXXXXXXXXXXXXXXXX

For all of you

Often practical, always sincere and heartfelt, James' letters are full of love for his family. This image shows the original letter dated 28 September 1917. Document from the collection of the Staffordshire Regiment Museum.

Fragment of unknown date

4 and 5 a week, so now you can best judge for yourself as to the time about that I shall be coming home, of course they may be increased in numbers or reduced we never know how many they are sending each week until the night before they go, they go every Thursday morning, I recon I shall about be home for my birthday. This is as much as I know about it at present, I am sorry we have got to wait so long darlings but it is so, and every week seems a year because we are all so anxious to see one another once more and have a sweet loving kiss from each others lips and our dear little ones, kiss the children for me and give my best wishes to all friends, we are having very nice weather out here just now, I hope Arthurs wife is still improving and the children going on alright and not giving you much trouble, chin up my darling the time will soon come when we shall be able to have a nice sweet kiss once again. It seems a long while to wait but it will soon pass over and then we shall have a very happy re-uniting so buck up your spirits and keep in good hopes as I know you will do. You're tired of it I know like myself but we cannot alter it now, so make the best of everything and make yourself as comfortable as possible until I come and then you shall have a good rest my flower, you shall not soil your hands during the time I am at home and shall be overjoyed to do it for you I will close now and wish you all good-day and god bless you with ever fondest love and dearest thoughts from your ever loving and faithful

Boy 'Jim'

I don't know if you will like the heading and tail of this letter by calling you my dear girl and me your boy but the reason is that I wanted to have a change in my letter to make it read a little bit different from the one thing that I keep sending to you my sweetheart, so I hope you will tell me if you like it or not best love from

Your true boy, husband and "Daddie"

XXXXXXXXXX for my sweet little ones from "Dad"

XXXXXXXXXX for my very own sweetheart from "Jim"

With best love for all.

James has been wounded...

23/10/17

Dear Mrs Stevenson

I went over to the No. 2 C.C.S. to see your husband yesterday and found him far more cheerful in himself, but still I am sorry to say dangerously ill. By this I do not mean you to give up hope, as while there is life there is hope; He was glad to get your message + is putting up a good fight + I trust he will with God's help pull through.

I will try to get over to see him again in a few days, when I will write to you again. God bless and strengthen you dear soul and remember – underneath all this are the everlasting Arms. Yours sincerely S.E.R. Jennings 9 N.S. Regt

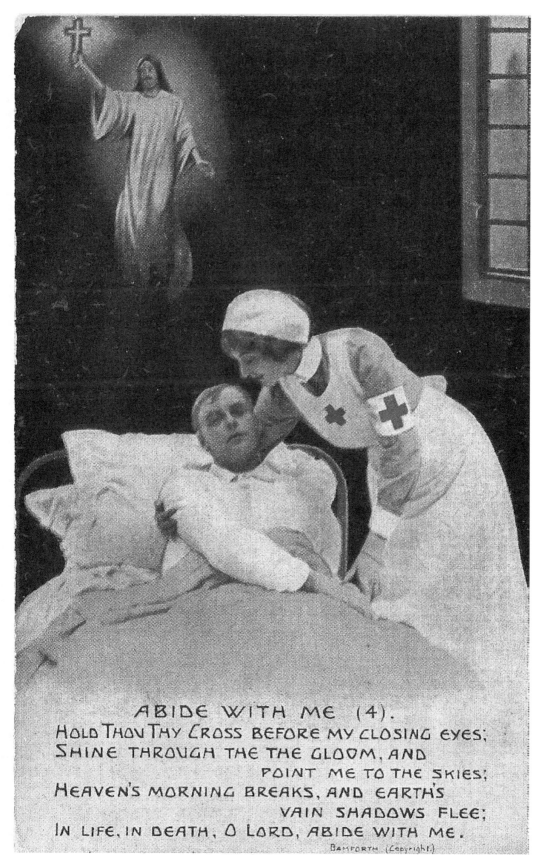

ABIDE WITH ME (4).
HOLD THOU THY CROSS BEFORE MY CLOSING EYES;
SHINE THROUGH THE THE GLOOM, AND
                    POINT ME TO THE SKIES;
HEAVEN'S MORNING BREAKS, AND EARTH'S
                    VAIN SHADOWS FLEE;
IN LIFE, IN DEATH, O LORD, ABIDE WITH ME.
BAMFORTH (Copyright.)

Bamforth song card

Oct 23

Dear Mrs Stevenson
I am sorry to tell you your husband is not so well as he was. The progress that he was making has not been maintained and he is very weak.
Everything possible is being done for him and he is a splendid patient. When possible he is carried out of the ward and lies in the sun. I will write again in a day or so. I wish I could give you better news.
Yours sincerely W Macleod

2 C.C.S.
24.10.17
I regret to say that Sgt Stevenson died this morning at 9. He was quite unconscious, and in no pain.
E M Hayes

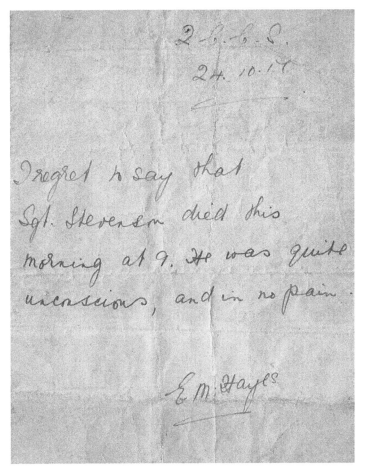

The original Casualty Clearing Station letter that first announced James' death dated 24 October 1917. Document from the collection of the Staffordshire Regiment Museum.

2 C.C.S BSF

24/10/17

Mr Dear Mrs Stevenson

I am very sorry to have to write to tell you bad news of your husband. He died this morning at 9am being quite unconscious and free from pain.

After I wrote yesterday I feared that he would not recover and trust that I prepared you by what I said.

I sent a message over this afternoon with some grapes for your husband (I was unable to go myself) and the enclosed note from the Sister was my confirmation that all was over with him.

My heart goes out in deepest sympathy for you + Officers and Men join me, all speaking so well of him, and saying what a loss he is to the Battalion.

I will see that a Regimental cross is erected on the grave which will be in Outtersteene cemetery.

God bless and comfort you and give you the absolute knowledge and assurance that Christ is with you both, binding you still by the unseen chains of his wonderful love.

Believe me, with deepest sympathy

Yours sincerely

S E R Jennings

C.F att d 9h Nth Sttfs Regt

2.C.C.S. Oct 25

Dear Mrs Stevenson

I am truly grieved to tell you that your husband has died of his wounds. The end came very peacefully [indecipherable word here] morning early. I am sorry that I was not there when he died but I believe he was unconscious for some time. It was always a great difficulty for him to speak.

He is buried in Outtersteene British Cemetery and a cross will be erected over his grave.

Please accept my deepest sympathy in your sorrow.

Yours sincerely W W Macleod

Letter fragment

I am a married man myself with two dear mites and all I pray for if I too must go to join the Sainted Martyrs who have already gone in this great strife after Right versus might, is that the [indecipherable] I love will be my dear Wife's comfort + support, the same as I pray he may be yours.

As you ask me I can tell you truthful the nature of his injuries.

The splinter of [indecipherable] caught him in the back (about half way down and towards the left side) just as he was returning to the tent after attending to some matters with the men of his platoon in their tents. All would have been well if the splinter had not penetrated to the lower part of his left lung which became septic and caused his death. If he had lived I am afraid he would have been a constant invalid and my dear friend you can thank God he was taken rather than that he should have been crippled all his life.

I must close with my deepest and heartfelt sympathy to you and your children.

The Lord God Bless you and keep you, his peace and presence comfort you.

Yours very sincerely L R Faresham

James' grave at Outtersteene Communal Cemetery with its Regimental cross. Image ©Staffordshire Regiment Museum.

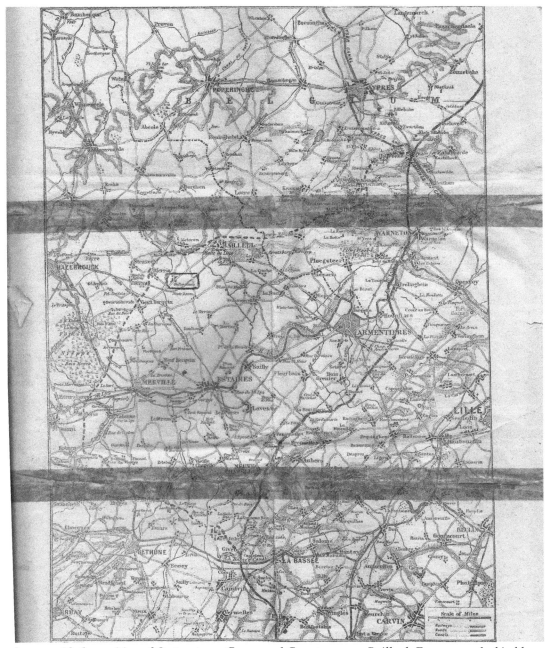

A map, with the position of Outtersteene Communal Cemetery near Bailleul, France, marked in blue ink by Eliza Stevenson.

James Stevenson died of his wounds on the 24th October aged 36. Relatives remember James Stevenson's daughter, Ada, who adored he father, talking about her mother (Eliza Stevenson) receiving the letter that first told her of her husband's death. Decades later tears would still come to her eyes.

Eliza Stevenson remarried and became Eliza Hibbert. She was still running Uncle Tom's Cabin as a public house in the 1930s. Eliza kept James' letters, his photograph, newspaper clippings and of course a photograph of his grave. Years later, the extreme fragility of these documents are a testament to how often they were read, and how carefully they were treasured.

Captain Reginald John Armes

Captain Reginald John (known as Jake) Armes was a Regular Officer of the 1st North Staffordshire Regiment. At the time of writing his letter home to his wife, he was 38 years old.

The 1911 Census gives his address as St Helen's, The Avenue, Camberley, Surrey. Captain Armes is listed as a Captain in the Infantry (Regular Army), who has been married to Eleonora Campbell (29) for five years. In 1911, they have one daughter Elizabeth Jean (3). Captain Armes (Jake) was born in Kings Lynn, Surrey and his wife in London. Their daughter however was born in Sutton Coldfield, suggesting the kind of moving about that the families of Army Officers had then and still do have to undertake. The household is listed as containing four servants – a cook, a nurserymaid, a parlourmaid and a housemaid. They are comfortably off.

On Christmas Eve 1914, along hundreds of miles of the Western Front approximately 100,000 Commonwealth and German forces spontaneously laid down their weapons for 48 hours. This famous truce allowed men from both sides to leave their trenches and meet each other as friends, albeit wary ones. The truce was initiated by the sound of troops from both sides singing into the night, by Christmas trees lit with small candles appearing in the German

Captain Armes

trenches and by brave individuals who walked out into No-Man's-Land to talk to the shadowy figures on the other side. Soon the truce spread. It allowed both sides to bury their dead, some of which had been lying in No-Man's-Land since October. The war had been in full fury for four months and already men were longing for home. The war would carry on for another four years.

All along the Front British, French, Belgian and German soldiers simply decided that for a few brief hours they would not contend with each other with weapons, but with songs, and in one reported case through a game of football (3-2 to the Germans). Germans held up signs inviting the British to impromptu concerts. Family photographs, even signet rings were exchanged and the killing stopped (although it must be mentioned that by no means did this happen across the whole Front, it was a miracle contained to the majority of the British Line and sections of the French and Belgian Line.) The truce lasted for two or three days in most places, but in some lasted until Boxing Day. There's also scattered evidence to suggest

Officers of the 1st Battalion North Staffordshire Regiment, Cambridge, August, 1914. Captain Armes is positioned in the first seated row, second from the left. From the collection of the Staffordshire Regiment Museum.

we fixed up that the men should not go near their opponents' trenches, but remain about midway between the lines. The whole thing is extraordinary. The men were all so natural and friendly. Several photos were taken, a group of German Officers, a German Officer and myself, and a group of British and German soldiers.

The Germans are Saxons, a good-looking lot, only wishing for peace in a manly way, and they seem in no way at their last gasp. I was astonished at the easy way in which our men and theirs got on with each other.

We have just knocked off for dinner, and have arranged to meet again afterwards until dusk when we go in again and have sleep until 9 p.m., when War begins again. I wonder who will start the shooting! They say "fire in the air and we will", and such things, but of course it will start and to-morrow we shall be at it hard killing one another. It is an extraordinary state of affairs which allows of a "Peace Day". I have never seen men so pleased to have a day off as both sides.

Their Opera Singer is going to give us a song or two to-night and perhaps I may give them one. Try and imagine two lines of trenches in peace, only 50 yards apart, the men of of either side have never seen each other except perhaps a head now and again, and

- 4 -

'Jake' Armes' letter dated 24 December 1914. From the collection of the Staffordshire Regiment Museum.

that a kind of truce existed in places until March and was in force again at Easter. Commanders of the British Armed Forces were aghast and horrified as news of the truce trickled back to England through the letters of those who took part, and names were demanded. No prosecutions ever took place.

Captain Armes survived both World Wars and died in 1948 at the age of 70. It's interesting to speculate on how many lives both he, his fellow officers and the men of the line were responsible for jointly saving. How many men would have died during those three days, who in actuality went on to survive, if fortunate, the rest of the conflict? Who knows, perhaps some of you reading this book may be alive due to the actions taken by Captain 'Jake' Armes on Christmas Eve 1914?

On December 24th 1914, near Ploegsteert, Captain 'Jake' Armes wrote home to his wife…

24/12/14

I have just been through one of the most extraordinary scenes imaginable. To-night is Xmas Eve and I came up into the trenches this evening for my tour of duty in them. Firing was going on all the time and the enemy's machine guns were at it hard, firing at us. Then about seven the firing stopped.

I was in my dug-out reading a paper and the mail was being dished out. It was reported that the Germans had lighted their trenches up all along our front. We had been calling to one another for some time Xmas wishes and other things. I went out and they shouted "no shooting" and then somehow the scene became a peaceful one. All our men got out of their trenches and sat on the parapet, the Germans did the same, and they talked to one another in English and broken English. I got on top of the trench and talked German and asked them to sign a German Volkslied [1], which they did, then our men sang quite well and each side clapped and cheered the other. I asked a German who sang a solo to sing one of Schumann's songs, so he sang "The Two Grenadiers" splendidly. Our men were a good audience and really enjoyed his singing.

Then Pope and I walked across and held a conversation with the German Officer in command. One of his men introduced us properly, he asked my name and then presented me to his officer. I gave the latter permission to bury some German dead who are lying in between us, and we agreed to have no shooting until 12 midnight to-morrow. We talked together, 10 or more Germans gathered round. I was almost in their lines within a yard or so. We saluted each other, he thanked me for permission to bury his dead, and we fixed up how many men were to do it, and that otherwise both sides must remain in their trenches.

Then we wished one another goodnight and a good night's rest, and a happy Xmas and parted with a salute. I got back to the trench. The Germans sang "Die Wacht Am

Rhein" [2] it sounded well. Then our men sang quite well "Christians Awake" [3], it sounded so well, and with a good night we all got back into our trenches. It was a curious scene, a lovely moonlit night, the German trenches with small lights on them, and the men on both sides gathered in groups on the parapets.

At times we heard the guns in the distance and an occasional rifle shot. I can hear them now, but about us is absolute quiet. I allowed one or two men to go out and meet a German or two half way. They exchanged cigars, a smoke and talked. The Officer I spoke to hopes we shall do the same on New Year's Day, I said "yes, if I am here." I felt I must sit down and write the story of this Xmas Eve before I went to lie down. Of course no precautions are relaxed, but I think they mean to play the game. All the same, I think I shall be awake all night so as to be on the safe side. It is weird to think that to-morrow night we shall be at it hard again. If one gets through this show it will be an Xmas time to live in one's memory. The German who sang had a really fine voice.

Am just off for a walk around the trenches to see all is well. Goodnight.

Xmas Day.

We had an absolutely quiet night in front of us though just to our right and left there was sniping going on. In my trenches and in those of the Enemy opposite to us were only nice big fires blazing and occasional songs and conversation. This morning at the Reveille the Germans sent out parties to bury their dead. Our men went out to help, and then we all on both sides met in the middle, and in groups began to talk and exchange gifts of tobacco, etc. All this morning we have been fraternising, singing songs. I have been within a yard in fact to their trenches, have spoken to and exchanged greetings with a Colonel, Staff Officers and several Company Officers. All were very nice and we fixed up that the men should not go near their opponents trenches, but remain about midway between the lines. The whole thing is extraordinary. The men were all so natural and friendly. Several photos were taken, a group of German Officers, a German Officer and myself, and a group of British and German soldiers.

The Germans are Saxons, a good looking lot, only wishing for peace in a manly way, and they seem in no way at their last gasp. I was astonished at the easy way in which our men and theirs got on with each other.

We have just knocked off for dinner, and have arranged to meet again afterwards until dusk when we go in again and have [sleep?] until 9pm, when War begins again. I wonder who will start the shooting! They say "Fire in the air and we will", and such things, but of course it will start and tomorrow we shall be at it hard killing one another. It is an extraordinary state of affairs which allows of a "Peace Day". I have never seen men so pleased to have a day off as both sides.

AROUND THE OLD CAMP FIRE (1).

'Tis midnight, and across the plain behold the British camp,
And in the silent night one hears the sentry's steady tramp,
And sons of England gather round the camp fire's steady
　　glow,
They sing a song of " Home, Sweet Home," it echoes o'er
　　the snow.

WORDS BY PERMISSION OF F. V. ST. CLAIR.
BAMFORTH Copyright

Bamforth song card

Their Opera Singer is going to give us a song or two tonight and perhaps I may give them one. Try and imagine two lines of trenches in peace, only 50 yards apart, the men of either side have never seen each other except perhaps a head now and again, and have never been outside in front of their trenches. Then suddenly one day men stream out and nest in friendly talk in the middle. One fellow, a married man, wanted so much a photo of Betty and Nancy in bed, which I had, and I gave him it as I had two: It seems he showed it all round, as several Germans told me afterwards about it. He gave me a photo of himself and family taken the other day which he had just got. Well must finish now so as to get this off to-day. Have just finished dinner. Pork chop. Plum pudding. Mince pies. Ginger, and bottle of Wine and a cigar, and have drunk to all at home and especially to you my darling one. Must go outside now to supervise the meetings of the men and the Germans.

Will try and write more in a day or two. Keep this letter carefully and send copies to all. I think they will be interested. It did feel funny walking over alone towards the enemy's trenches to meet someone half-way, and then to arrange a Xmas peace. It will be a thing to remember all one's life.

Kiss the babies and give them my love. Write me a long letter and tell me all the news. I hope the photos come out all-right. Probably you will see them in some paper. Yours, [Signed] Jake.

28/12/14

Last night when sitting in my dug-out in the fire trenches, I got a wire to say I had been made a Staff Officer and was to report myself as soon as possible, so here I am. My address will now be:-

H.Q's 2nd Army,

Brit. Exp. Force.

Please note not 11 Army or Army Corps.

Just as we were finishing our meal last night there was a tremendous explosion and flash. It fairly shook the place. We could not make it out at first it seemed so close. We discovered that the Germans had blown up a house about 200 yards [indecipherable]

I was very sad at leaving the Company this morning. I got quite a lump at my throat as I went round the trench and shook hands with them all. We have been through the mill together and fought side by side. They seemed grieved to lose me, which made it worse. I do not feel I can say much about it.

Please send me out my brown brogues and also ask Harrods about the cigars [4], they never came.

I left our friends of Xmas Day in a quiet mood. I stood upon the parapet and had a final look round, and not a shot was fired. I will write more of this later.

Notes
1. Volkslied – German for folk song.
2. Die Wacht Am Rhein is a German patriotic song that translates as 'The watch in the Rhine'. It was particularly popular during WW1. Translated, the lyrics are:

The Guard on the Rhine

A cry roars out like echoing thunder.
Like rattling of swords, like foaming waves.
Onwards to the Rhine, to the Rhine, the German Rhine.
Who wants to be guardian of the stream?

Dear Fatherland, you may be assured,
The guard on the Rhine remains steadfast and loyal.
Firm and true stand the watch on the Rhine.
Firm and true stand the watch on the Rhine.

Through hundreds, thousands the call flashes through,
And all their eyes shine bright.
The German youth, faithful and strong,
Guards the German borderland.

He looks towards the heaven's blue,
Where his heroic fathers look down,
And swears with proud vigilance,

Rhine, you will remain German like my breast!

While still remains one breath of life,
While still one fist can draw a knife,
One gun still fired with one hand,
No foe will stand on this Rhine sand.

And even if my heart breaks in death,
You will never become foreign territory.
Rich, as your flood is with water,
Germany is with heroes' blood!

The oath rings out, the wave runs,
The banners waving high in the wind,
On the Rhine, on the Rhine, on the German Rhine,
We all want to be your guardians.

So lead us on, you are wise,
Trusting in Good, take your sword,
Hail Wilhelm! Down with all that brood!
And repay our shame with the foe's blood.

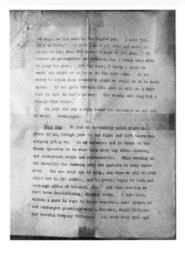
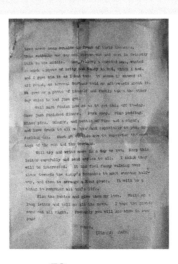

Captain Armes'
original letter

3. In response the British sang 'Christians awake, salute the happy morn.'

Christians awake, salute the happy morn.

Christians, awake, salute the happy morn,
Whereon the Saviour of the world was born.
Rise to adore the mystery of love,
Which hosts of angels chanted from above.
With them the joyful tidings first begun,
Of God incarnate and the virgin's son.

Then to the watchful shepherds it was told,
Who heard the angelic herald's voice, Behold,
I bring good tidings of a Saviour's birth,
To you and all the nations of the earth.
This day hath God fulfilled His promised Word,
This day is born a Saviour, Christ the Lord.

He spoke; and straight-away the celestial choir,
In hymns of joy, unknown before, conspire,
The praises of redeeming love they sang,
And Heav'n's whole orb with allelulias rang.
God's highest glory was their anthem still,

Peace on the earth and unto men good will.

To Bethlehem straight the enlightened shepherds ran,
To see the wonder God had wrought for man,
And found, with Joseph and the blessed maid,
Her son, the Saviour, in a manger laid.
Then to their flocks, still praising God, return,
And their glad hearts with holy rapture burn.

Like Mary let us ponder in our mind,
God's wondrous love in saving lost mankind,
Trace we the babe, who hath retrieved our loss,
From His poor manger to His bitter cross.
Tread in His steps, assisted by His grace,
Till man's first heavenly state again takes place.

Then may we hope, the angelic hosts among,
To sing, redeemed, a glad triumphal song,
He that was born upon this joyful day,
Around us all His glory shall display.
Saved by His love, incessantly we sing,
Eternal praise to Heaven's almighty king.

4. It was quite usual for 'high-end' retailers such as Harrods and Fortnum and Mason to send items directly to officers in the trenches. Items such as potted shrimp, cigars and socks etc would arrive regularly.

Second-Lieutenant Alfred Bull, 3rd Battalion South Staffordshire Regiment

Alfred Bull. Image from the collection of the Staffordshire Regiment Museum

Dam Street, Lichfield. Number 27 is the red brick building on the far right-hand side of the picture. It is just a short way away from Lichfield Cathedral and Quonians Lane.

Alfred Bull was born and lived most of his life at number 27 Dam Street, Lichfield. He was a Master stone and woodcarver at the famous Lichfield firm of architectural stonemasons Robert Bridgman and Sons. The following is his first-hand account of his experiences during WW1. He was a strong minded and hugely capable man who also served during WW2, but that story will have to wait for another book!

Alfred was born in 1896 and died in 1989. He had two brothers, William and Francis. The 1911 census lists the household at number 27 Dam Street as William Bull (43), a woodcarver from Worcester, Ada Bull (42) who was born in Lichfield as were William and Ada's three sons William (18), a woodcarver, Frank 16, a bookseller and Alfred (14), also listed as a woodcarver.

Alfred married Avis Alice George in 1920 and they had a son three years later who they named Ralph.

Dennis Parsons MBE, renowned Master carver and sculptor had this to say about Alfred...

"Alfred, known as Alf, was a very good wood and stone foliage carver whose work can be seen in many cathedrals, churches and stately homes throughout the length and breadth of the country.

"He was employed by the well know ecclesiastic and architectural company Robert Bridgeman and was their foreman carver, as was his father before him. He was a strict disciplinarian but one of the fairest men I have ever known, standing up for

This image shows the workshops and offices of Robert Bridgeman & Sons on Quonians Lane. Robert Bridgeman & Sons, the highly regarded firm of architectural and ecclesiastical stonemasons, had their workshops here from the late 19th century, and it is here that Alf, his father and brother worked. Sculptor Robert Bridgeman came to Lichfield in 1877 to work on Lichfield Cathedral and he is responsible for many of the remarkable figures on the West Front. The 1881 census shows Robert as living on Dam Street, where he would have been a neighbour of the Bull family.

both his workmen and the management whenever occasion demanded.

"He was also a well respected member of local society standing on various charitable committees. His other interests were theatre, horse racing, reading and best of all his garden."

The following is a first-hand account that was given by Alfred in 1985. As you can hear, he was as concise and straightforward in his ninth decade as he was at the age of 18.

Recollections Of The First World War

By 2nd Lieutenant Alfred Charles Bull 3rd Battalion South Staffordshire Regiment

Joined forces June 17th, 1915, when I was 18 and a half years old. Went to Drill Hall, Burton on Trent[1] in private billets. Six months basic training (square bashing) and field work on Bass's Meadow.[2] Marched 27 miles lunchtime to Rugeley Market Hall[3] – then across Shugborough Park to Tixall. Four of us started to play football. The Regt. Sergeant Major said "If you can play football after that you can do a guard." We all had stripes the next week.[4]

I was sent with six men to be attached to the Northumberland Fusiliers for training on machine guns.[5] In a large camp at Gateshead in tents with thousands of men. Our instructor was Sgt. Wright. A long march to musketry camp at Whitley Bay – the Fifth North had sent a Sergeant and six men. He left everything to me. A few weeks and another six men arrived – some from the 5th and I was made a full Corporal.

The 5th had sent an Officer this time and he was like the Sergeant (no good). The Northumberlands refused to ration us except Army issue. This meant we supplied our own cooks and we had two pence ha'penny a day to spend on such things as jam and that sort of thing. Again everything was left to me, but I made the officer sign for all the things I bought (I was pleased about this afterwards when we re-joined our own battalion and it all had to be squared up with the Quarter Master.)

A few days before Xmas 1915 we had orders to return to Unit and I wrote to the Adjutant for Xmas leave. On Xmas Eve I was called to the Orderly Room when I drew my four days pass book, pay, etc. I learned that I was now a sergeant, dated November, which made me war substantive rank. I was just 19 and a very experienced soldier. I had been away for nearly five months with 26 men and not one on a charge.[6]

The Battalion was now at Belton Park, Grantham – about the worst camp in Britain – in huts on a mud heap.

Bill and Frank my brothers, were on draught leave, so we were all at home that Xmas,

The Town Hall, Rugeley. Image from the collection of The Landor Society, Rugeley.

The Market Place, Rugeley. Image from the collection of The Landor Society, Rugeley.

the last time for some years.

I returned to the sixth North and was an all-round instructor at the time when the Bevan Boys [7] were being called up. On guard at the Arsenal [8] in Grantham one night (locked in and no one allowed in or out after dark) there was a big fire at the leather factory two miles away – sparks and smoke all night and we did not know what we guarded.

I was sent to Derby to take over billet for the company (advance party). Slept on the floor in a Billiards Room at the Cavendish Hotel, on the corner of Normandy Road.

Took over the St Albans School. A new Colonel who striped all the sergeants or sent them abroad. We were reduced to seven men in our training battalion which meant orderly once a week and guard once a week – attend all parades and instruct recruits.

I was put on a charge, absent from parade. I was at Company Orderly Room with Company Commander and supposed to be at Co. Orderly Rooms over a mile away at the same time. Charge sheet was torn up and Co. Orderly Room time allowed.

A gale blew the telephone poles down on the Loughborough Road and I took a detail out for about two weeks to help the telephone men with the repairs. The men were from the Overseas Company and we got on well.

I had never been on an Instructors Course and, after complaining to the Co. Officer, was sent on a six weeks course to Fulford Barracks, York. Result was three goods and a very good recommendation for P.T. and musketry which meant they had to send me to Aldershot or Strensall. Went on P.T. course at Aldershot. The battalion had moved to Catterick (we were some of the first troops there) I enjoyed P.T. with lots of recruits. We sent a 300 draught to re-enforce the 5th and 6th North, who had got caught at Gommecourt. Nearly all these men were killed within 10 days on the Somme. Mervin Larkin and one of the Horobins were in the draught. [9]

At the end of the summer we moved to Lincoln and trained on the racecourse there. I claimed four days leave and when I got back found myself on draught for overseas with train loads of men. This was my first time to France.

In November, 1916 [10] I was recommended for commission and came back to England in April, 1917. In France for my 20th birthday. Went up the line in cattle trucks - two days and nights spent mostly being shunted about in Abbeville with re-enforcements for the 8th North. Joined them at Lonseballite a village near Dorillers. My number was now 40796.

Personal No 14 1162

Surname **BULL**

Christian Names **ALFRED CHARLES**

Date of Birth _November 21st 1896_

Regiment _South Staffordshire (Temporary)_

NOTE.—~~State~~ whether commission is ~~Regular, Special Reserve, Territorial,~~ or Temporary. The number of the battalion is on no account to be stated.

Permanent Home Address _27 Dam St Lichfield_

Civil Profession or Occupation before the War } _Wood Carver_

Agents _Messrs Cox & Co Charing Cross_

Full Name and Address of Next-of-Kin

Albert William Bull 27 Dam St Lichfield.

2

Alf's Army Pay Book. Document from the collection of the Staffordshire Regiment Museum.

These are things I recall and little incidents which happened to me. Was put in charge of no.4 platoon, A Coy. at the end of November. The battalion had been badly cut up on the Somme and Christmas parcels were coming for men who were either dead or wounded. We, the Sergeants, had to open them and hand on letters to be answered by Officers. [11] The contents were distributed. We went up the line in trucks and finished up in Courville, a village behind the line but not far. Into the third line at Helentown, this is where I really went to war. The first night a shell killed four men in Sgt. Pepper's platoon and Pep and I had to sort out the discs and pay books. I had never seen a corpse before. The fumes of the shells and blood got me in the stomach and gave me the runs for some time. [12]

However, I had other things to think about. Sergeant Pepper and I were firm friends and mucked in together. He was not very big but a very brave man – used bad language and a born leader. We were pals from the start.

There was a large pool in the centre at Hebutown and the Germans dropped a salvo of shells on it every so often. We used to wait for them and the water to settle and then move past.

My first visit to the front line was to take a ration party [13] who had turned back three times because of shelling. A Sergeant had to take them and of course we had to cut the cards to see who. Naturally or by design it was me. But by this time it had quietened down. The communication trench was so full of mud and water and the men so loaded, I ordered them up on top. We had an easy journey and very quick too.

The front line was not a continuous trench, [14] but platoon posts every forty yards or so. Relief was a lot different too. An officer and four men came up and took over the posts and the company left to make way for the incoming company to occupy later.

One day we were relieved and finished up in about three days in a bivouac in a sunken road. About four o'clock in the night we were taken away-finishing up on the side of the road to get what sleep we could before dawn.

The next morning I was detailed to take four men and a guide to take over the St Quentin front from the Australians.[15] They cleared out smartly their officer's orders being obeyed without question promptly. That's how we came to St Quentin canal front. I still have a lead figure of a saint I picked up in that trench. In and out of that part of the line for weeks until February. I learned about patrols and outposts. One night the company officer must have had a tip from somewhere – we were told to load up and the whole company was to go forward (this was at Stand 2 before the rations came up). In Open Order we went forward by moonlight - must have got nearly a mile and never a shot fired. Settled for the night in slit trenches – sat on one another's knees, head buried in the back of the man in front. Call for platoon commanders – told we were lost in No Man's Land. It was decided to move forward again at daybreak, until we got fired on.

First shot and we went to earth in an old German Trench (the filthiest I have ever been in). Got one foot stuck and could have cried. By the time I had dug it free the other was stuck. [16]

My stretcher bearers were Mason and Benton, Mason carried a man back to find a doctor, who said the man could have walked back. Mason got back and brought four or five small loaves which I broke up among the men. I never had a bit of it myself. This was our second day and night without food or sleep.

We decided that the place in front of us was Pouleux. We were told to make our way back to where we had started from. Here we had rations and time to sleep.
This was where my platoon found some bottles of wine that had been lost or dumped. Mason was blind drunk and I thumped him and threatened him, but could not keep him quiet.

The C.O. sent for me. I told him that I had all the rum I wanted, but they wouldn't tell me where it was. Everyone to dug-out except the sentry and his mate. Next morning Lt. Bell was taken to the rum and all was forgiven.

		SERVICE.						
AT HOME			ABROAD					
Unit.	From	To	With an Expedy. Fee.		Elsewhere		Wounded (date)	Sick (date)
			From	To	From	To		
6rn North Staffs	17/6/15	17/11/16						
8 rn North Staffs	18/11/17	31/10/17	18/11/16	17/4/17				
South Staffs	21/10/17	9/1/18	10/1/18	27/3/18			23/3/18	
	28/3/18	19/7/18	20/7/	8/9/18			3/10/18	
	9/10/18	26/1/19						
14th South Staffs	31/7/40	26/11/40						
1/9 South Staffs	27/11/40	18/6/41						
5th SWB	14/6/41	6/10/41						

Showing Alf's Army service from 17 June 1915 right through to 6 October 1941. Document from the collection of the Staffordshire Regiment Museum.

After four days doing working parties with R.E.s we started the long march to Belgium.

While on the Somme for a time we had as our temporary Colonel D E Wyatt, V.C; one arm and one eye. In the second war he was a Brigadier and served in Norway with the Para troopers there. Later he was in the desert with General Robertson. The yarn was that he wanted to be killed in action.

Our march to Belgium finished at Diche Beach, where the lines were very close – we looked back on Remal Hill.

It was after this that I came home for a commission. Pepper soon followed me. When he went out again I heard that he was killed within a week.

My adventures the third time out to France ended the war for me after St Quentin with a bullet through my left arm at Woraceguin Hill.

First I must explain how I was with Bates and the fourth South Staffords in March, 1918 and the German advance on Paris, I was only in just three days.

When it started to rain shells and machine gun fire 2nd Lt. Bates was roaming round looking for trouble. He did not know the meaning of fear and was a rough merchant. When I went out the third time we were at Calais together. One day in the mess he came in wearing a couple of medals – the French and Belgian Croix de Guerre. This was the first time I knew him for one of the War Heroes. It turned out he had been recommended for the V.C. three times, the only medal he wanted but never got.

If anyone was to get into trouble it was to be the expendables like Bates and Bull. There was trouble with some 51st Division Jocks who refused to go up the line – a little mutiny and they were going to pay a visit to Provo Marshall, who had one of their men in custody. Bates was acting Captain now and he was detailed to stop them.

The main road into Calais was over a small bridge and another bridge on a minor road. Why I was put in charge of this second bridge I never knew, but think Bates had something to do with it. Anyway they did not come my way and a Staff Officer took away Bates' Lewis gun. The Jocks went up the line next day like lambs. Bates and I went up the line to the 5th S. Staffords. The Battalion were in front of Bethune and things were very different from being on the Somme.

A miniature railway took rations up the line and the track was hit by a shell – it was quickly replaced by spares. It was more open country with acres of wheat. This was where we did daylight patrols. An officer and a man were all day in No Man's Land on company fronts.

My first term in the front line was very eventful and gave me confidence which I never lost afterwards.

The relief of the front line company went smoothly, but an hour or so later we got shelled badly. I was at the head of the communication trench and one of my platoon (a boy about my own age) came scrambling saying he was going home or something. I threatened him and eventually two men sat on him to keep him quiet.

Shelling eased off but there was hell to play on our left and looking over that was about 200 yards I saw a thing that made me laugh. A pack mule had got lose and any time a shell got near him he lay down and then was up and off again.

It was the only time I had a platoon officer in the line.

His name was Poizer and I saw little of him – but he was all right and knew his job. The weather was awful and we wore thigh boots. Rain, snow, frost sometimes. We looked like snowmen covered in rime from top to toe.

September 29th, 1985. [17]

Today 67 years ago the Staffordshire Brigade broke the Hindenburg Line and brought the First World War end in sight.

I was one of the leaders that morning. I volunteered to take the place of a 2nd. Lieutenant who had no experience. I should have been on echelon B that day attached to headquarters. We two, 2nd Lieutenant Jones and myself wrote letters to be sent home if we got killed, which was quite expected to happen. No one expected us to be successful and see another day.

We gave the "over the top" signal. The fog was so thick it saved our lives. We had very few casualties and everything went according to plan. The only attack in the First World War when everything went right and those letters were never posted. I wonder if long Jones and short Jones are alive today? How I came to volunteer is a separate story.

To take and break the Hindenburg Line at any point seemed an impossible task for any troops. So when we were facing the St. Quentin Canal advance we knew what it

An exploding mine. Image © Staffordshire Regiment Museum.

meant. Two thousand yards of the most heavily armed ground and the canal itself was a formidable task. We knew that it was almost certain death and no glory. We were to go over on the morning of Sept. 29th.

On the 27th I was called to a company conference. The captain of our company was to go on leave on the 28th (he was a brave man who had been with the battalion a long time and they did not wish to lose him. This is my view of the circumstances). On the 29th I should have been on echelon 13 for the day and everyone knew this. It was put to me that the skipper could not go on leave unless I volunteered to go over. With four other officers looking at you what answer can you give? [18]

1) The transit camp at Calais was made up of bell tents [19] with a hut that was the Officer's mess. One night a severe gale brought them all down except mine, which was a wreck but still standing. There I was; two 6th North Staffords from Lichfield, Tony Russell and George Chapman – a fitter from Barnards Levett in Bird Street – had not a sou between them, so I gave them a few francs as a latch lifter to get into the canteen. One day a little fighter plane came down a little way from where I was. It tipped on its nose and the pilot, a Frenchman, crawled out unhurt. He just walked away is if nothing had happened.

2) On the Somme at that time was a series of Platoon posts connected by some false trenches about six inches deep which photographed like the real thing from the air. A large shell came over. I could tell it would drop about sixty yards behind and watched it land. I saw a man's body go up about twenty feet in the air, spinning like a Catherine wheel – arms and legs spread – it seemed to pause at the top and still spinning. It was nothing to do with me.

3) Another time it was very quiet and a nice summer day. The company cooks made a dug out their home about a hundred yards behind. They must have been careless and made a lot of smoke. A German plane came over and dropped a couple of small bombs which made a direct hit. We were on short rations borrowed from other companies that day.

4) There was a foot or more of snow on the Somme and an officer – first time out – was given to Pepper's platoon. One bright moonlit night he got Pep to take him on patrol. They went out a few hundred yards and he lay taking compass bearings. The conversation went like this: - Officer "I think I've been far enough." Sgt. Pepper "You bloody fool! We haven't passed our outposts yet." [20]

5) When I was at home I picked up a paper one day. It showed a half naked soldier supposedly reading the 'Mirror'. But on looking closer he was delousing his shirt.

6) After our long march from the Somme to Belgium we landed in the front line at Dickie Beach in front of Kemmet Hill. The trenches here were only fifty or sixty yards apart. It was a very hot spot and the trenches were built up with water just below the surface. One day I changed my socks – they had been changed several times before – but at least they were dry. I went along on trench patrol, trod on a duck board that was loose and it let me into the water – my fault and my feet were as wet as ever. One night we took over the second line and the Germans strafed the front line with mortars – the best firework display I had ever seen. I sat on the top and watched it. Returned to my bivouac and found a man who had run away from it – a deserter from the front line. When things quietened down I took him back to his own company or I would have been a witness at a court-martial on a shooting charge. This was my last trip up the line as a Sergeant.

7) The day we had taken St. Quentin Canal I was bending down taking particulars of casualties when a shell came through the parapet and took a piece out of it. When I stood up straight I could see the gaps in it both ways. Luckily it was a dud but it could have taken my head straight off. Going back I stood talking to the runner I had with me when an IO6 fuse which was quite harmless went off between my feet. Quickly dismissing my runner I made for an old German gun pit and sat and cursed for a few minutes. Anyway I was soon back to normal and as good as ever.
I never found out what an IO6 fuse was – but they suddenly went off like a small firework and left a stain on the ground for a few moments.

Notes

1. This Drill Hall was in a building that formerly housed a skating rink in 1900 at the South End of Burton Meadow, or Alfred could have been referring to a building on Horninglow Street, behind the Magistrates Court that was also used as a Drill Hall by 1915.

2. Square Bashing, or drilling, taught a soldier and a unit to obey commands within seconds and without thought. This quick reaction time could save your life when in a combat situation. Drills might include arms drill, bayonet cleaning, platoon drill, kit inspection or a dozen other things. It is very hard to point your gun at another human being and fire it. Drill might save your life by eliminating that split second of indecision.

3. Rugeley Market Hall. See page 85.

4. In other words, they'd all been promoted and now wore Corporal's 'stripes' on their uniforms.

5. Alf is chosen for Machine Gun training. This is a responsible job that needs nerves of steel and the ability to concentrate, aim and stay in position when the rest of your unit may be falling back. Already at 18 Alf is proving himself to be an unusual man.

Interestingly, in 1914 the Belgian army used specially trained dog teams to pull the gun carriages of their machine guns. The breed used for this (and other jobs, including pulling up to 200 lbs of ammunition) were Belgian Mastiffs, a large breed that were both more hardy and economical than horses. They were also lower to the ground so less likely to be hit in combat, and were so well trained that they would stay quiet and still in the most terrifying circumstances. Dogs were also used as 'Mercy Dogs' to bring medical supplies to men who had been injured and were lying in No Man's Land. Often, it would be impossible for stretcher bearers to get to these men, and the dogs were trained to take small packages of medical supplies to the wounded (bandages etc.), or if the man was too severely wounded to help himself, to sit with him until he was found or died. By 1918 the combined British Allied and German Allied forces had employed over 50,000 dogs. Two breeds that were particularly used were Dobermans and German Shepherds. Dogs were used as scouts and sentries. Terriers were also used to clear some of the rats from the trenches and as Mascots. Perhaps one of the most remarkable uses that dogs were put to was as messengers. A training school to train messenger dogs was set up in Scotland, and one of its dogs travelled over 4,000 metres over terrible terrain along the Western Front with an important message. It did so in 1 hour when all other methods of getting the message through had failed.

6. Alf had kept his 26 men in good order, no one had got into trouble for anything. He is still only 18 years old.

7. The Bevin Boys were groups of young men conscripted into Mining during WW2,

L. V. C

EN GUERRE
MITRAILLEUSES BELGES.

THE WAR. BELGIAN MACHINE-GUNS.

In 1914 the Belgian Army used a hardy breed of mastiff to pull their machine guns.

it's possible that Alf is referring here to miners being conscripted into the Army, as they were in their thousands during WW1 to join the 'Moles'. These enormously brave men would be at work in the Front Lines, tunnelling from the British trenches towards the German lines where they would lay explosives directly underneath to destroy the enemy's trench. The dangers of this sort of job were manifold, not only could you be asphyxiated or blown up by carbon monoxide and other gas build-up underground, but the German's were also tunnelling towards the British lines. If two shafts met, as they often did, men would find themselves fighting underground with knives in a collapsing tunnel.

8. The Arsenal Alf is referring to would have been a weapons holding store, full of shells, bombs, bullets etc. Just one spark could have taken out the store and a lot of the surrounding area. It's interesting to note that this store was in a civilian area, close to many of the ammunition factories.

9. Alf's energy levels are getting him noticed again and he is now a Physical Training Instructor. During WW1 it was noticed that many of the men who were expected to fight were of poor physical condition. This of course is due to so many of them growing up in polluted cities where there was no national health system and rickets and Tuberculosis were rife. It's thought that the 1920s 'keep young and beautiful' obsession with the perfect physical form was a result of this realisation. In 1915, the size of the average British soldier was 5 feet 5 inches. The Germans were on average 5 feet 6 inches.

This image shows Tunstall in 1910 and gives a very good idea of the kind of polluted environment working people had to put up with.

10. The Battle of the Somme started on 1st July 1916 and carried on until November of the same year, when Alf was recommended for a commission. On the first day of the Somme, more men were killed or injured in 24 hours than ever before or since. There were nearly 60,000 casualties created on 1st July 1916, of these nearly 20,000 were killed.

11. It was the Officer's grim task to write letters home to the family, confirming the death of their loved one. I've read many over the course of this book. There are very few that seem to be written to a formula or without care. The handwriting may be terrible, due to lack of sleep etc., but each seems sincere enough in its way. Letters from the WW1 period, written 'in the field' are almost uniformly written in pencil. This is because a pencil will write on wet paper, a fountain pen won't. You can also sharpen a snapped pencil but a broken or rusty pen is useless. Officially, parcels were to be simply returned unopened, with the terse comment 'Killed in Action' written on them. Sometimes the parcel would arrive home, battered and dirty and bearing that dreadful news before the official letter arrived.

12. If you have ever been close to a dead animal that has been killed on the road, you'll have some idea of the smell that Alf is referring to. The corpses that Alf had to move would already have been decomposing. Often these corpses would swell with gasses that had built up in the stomach cavity. It would then burst, giving off a repulsive stench. It's the kind of smell that sticks to you, and you don't seem to be able to get out of your nose. Imagine being on the Somme, where thousands of bodies still lay, rotting and prey to scavenging animals. The smell of death and decay is rancidly sweet, vaguely like pickle mixed with human excrement and sour milk. Of course, eventually, you get used to even this, and there are accounts of soldiers moving slimy corpses all day and then eating without even stopping to wash their hands. Syd Norton also complains to Fan about the nausea caused by this task. The 'smell of the shells' that Alf refers to was the chemical stink of the cordite used to propel the shell.

If new trenches were being built on the site of an old battle, then you would be quite likely to unearth liquefying bodies as you dug down. These are the kind of sights that never left you, and must have made it almost impossible to reintegrate into society after the war, when those who loved you had no idea of what you had seen, and how it had changed you. What a heart-breaking position to be in…to desperately need comfort but be unable to get it.

In addition to the smell of decomposing corpses and the latrines, the men themselves would smell of sweat and unwashed feet. The trench would reek of the chloride of lime powder that was sprinkled around as a general disinfectant, plus cordite from spent shells, gas, rotting materials, cigarette smoke and cooking food. It was an aroma all of its own. In the collection of the Staffordshire Regiment Museum is an old piece of duckboard transformed by an enterprising soldier with a few spent bullet cases and a bit of wire into a telephone exchange board. The thought occurred to me that the spongey old wood, that is still scattering dried mud, might retain some of the smell of the trenches. It did.

A highly ingenious telephone switchboard made from old trench duckboards, the metal band from an ammunition box, a little bit of wire and a handful of spent bullet casings. This remarkable artefact still retains some of the unique smell of the trenches. Artefact from the Staffordshire Regiment Museum collection.

Rats were a major problem and trenches were infested with both black and brown rats. A rat can have up to 900 offspring in a year and the trenches were a great place to find food, with the eyes and livers of corpses particularly favoured. Some black rats could grow up to the size of a cat and would slither across soldiers when they were sleeping or on duty. Frogs and mice also bred in the trenches and water filled shell holes, and slugs and beetles were everywhere.

13. Alf regularly gets the hardest jobs and being in the ration party was one of the hardest. Not only would a party of men have to leave the trench and cover open ground in order to get behind the lines to collect the men's rations (thereby making themselves the target of every available gun) they would then have to clamber heavily laden with water, tins etc. back again, and maybe repeat this several times. Casualty rates within ration parties were extraordinarily high.

14. A quick note on how the front lines were laid out.

In many cases, the front lines weren't well dug and designed trenches but just a series of shell holes that men would rush into and try to extend when the shelling let up. This meant that these shell holes would not be linked back to safe areas via trenches that took them out of main firing range. To get back to gather rations, deliver messages, be relieved or relieve another set of men or simply move where requested would require negotiating churned, pitted and above all open ground close to the enemy's guns. This would often have been attempted under cover of darkness, and so night time was when the firing rose in intensity. The night could be one long deafening roar of fire and death, interspersed with daytimes that were often monotonous and dull. This was enormously bad for men's nerves, alternating times of terror with times of boredom in which to contemplate the terror. Many got used to it, and barely flinched at the sound of a bullet or shell, realising that flinching would make no difference to your prospects of survival. Those who didn't adapt suffered crippling anxiety and Post Traumatic Stress Disorder. One of the ways that men reported alleviating their terror mid-bombardment was to repeat a sequence of words or actions. This might be the lyrics of a song or a sequence of numbers. You might beat a tattoo on the floor of the trench whilst keeping your head pressed to the ground or the wall. Robert Graves remembers repeating the opening line of a Music Hall song "Oh I do like a s'nice s'mince pie" again and again. It worked.

15. Alf is talking here about moving forward to relieve the Australian troops who were defending a section of the front line at St Quentin Canal. This meant the Australians were moving back while Alfred and his battalion moved forward. As happened so often they got lost in a terrain that had no distinguishing features. Later in his account, Alf talks about The Battle of St Quentin Canal (that happened some weeks later after his Battalion had been in position for a while). It was a combined attack by British, American and Australian forces against the Germans. It was such a ferocious and concerted attack that the Hindenburg Line was breeched for the first time. (See point 14 of Alf's account). It is regarded as the pivotal point in the war as this defeat convinced the German High Command that a German victory was now very unlikely. Alf is talking here about the beginning of the battle, when he and his company were ordered forward. After that night of sitting, cramped on each other's knees, they found that they were lost in No Man's Land, cut off from the rest of the Battalion. This was very easily done and many soldiers greatly feared becoming lost, wandering alone until you were picked off. Alf is in the midst of a battlefield that has been razed of any distinguishing features, not a tree, bush or building anywhere for as far as the eye can see and all a uniform shade of mud.

16. At daybreak, the battle begins and they are forced into a German trench. It must have been basically an open cess pit. The mud and filth churned up to a viscous clinging mass that you sank in up to your knees and had to dig each foot out of. Being trapped, unable to move as the bullets flew must have been appalling. No book on WW1 is complete without a description of

Showing a supply convoy going through hell and high-water (quite literally) to keep supplies coming in. The supply party would also bring the post, handing out letters and parcels and any news that was circulating. It kept those held 'up the line' sane to have someone new to talk to occasionally and stopped any feeling of isolation.

one of the endemic problems of the soldier – mud. Sidney Rogerson tells us of the mud on the Somme that "It was like walking through caramel. At every step the foot stuck fast, and was only wrenched out by a determined effort, bringing away with it several pounds of earth till legs ached in every muscle."

17. On this day in 1918, Allied forces broke through the Hindenburg Line (known to the Germans as the Siegfried Line). This Line was the German's 'line in the sand' - their last line of defence. It consisted of a formidably defended line that ran from Northern France to Belgium, bristling with barbed wire and artillery. The St Quentin Canal was on this line.

The battle of St Quentin Canal was part of the "Hundred Days Offensive" that started in August 1918. Australian, American, French and British forces were involved in a massive attack that saw 1,637 guns firing at 10,000 feet of the Hindenburg Line. The Allies rained down thousands of shells and the line was broken on the 29th September. The Germans retreated in complete disarray. At home in Germany, Kaiser Wilhelm was being pushed into political reform by the Armed Forces, and their allies and Bulgaria were agitating for an Armistice. As the Allies moved forward, the Kaiser and his supporters realised that victory was impossible and WW1 came to a close on November 11th 1918.

18. Reading between the lines, it seems likely that the Company Captain was nearing breaking point and in need of a few days out of the firing line. The suggestion seems to be that if he didn't go, the company would 'lose him'. In order for him

to be still granted his pass, another man would have to step up. Alfred did so.

There were several reasons why a man might be sent out under cover of darkness to crawl over No-Man's-Land towards the enemy's trenches. In this case, the men are on patrol, trying to catch a glimpse of where the enemy's barbed wire is, what lies ahead of them, where the Sentries are etc. Crawling a very short distance could take hours as Sentries would be straining for any movement out in the darkness, and could send up a flare if they wanted a better look. It was extraordinarily dangerous. Men would come back (if they came back at all) sweating and shaking with exhaustion and nerves. Also, both British and German forces would launch 'trench raids', usually under the cover of darkness. This would necessitate one or two men crawling across No Man's Land to drop, silently, and usually at night into their opponent's trench where they would kill as many sleeping or unaware men as they could. The weapons of choice for these raids were knives or 'trench clubs' that could kill with as little noise as possible. It must have made for very uneasy sleep and a long night of watchfulness.

Trenches were officially marked on maps using a numerical system. When you were in the rabbit warren however, it was useless to try and navigate by numbers that were not in any case shown anywhere in the trench. Soldiers therefore named them themselves by either landmarks from back home, such as Piccadilly, or by any distinguishing feature, leading to names such as 'Dead Hun Corner'. This spot would be would be marked, of course, by a

Army Form Z. 3

☞ **IF FOUND, please drop this Certificate in a Post Office letter box.**

Notice.—"This document is Government property. It is no security whatsoever for debt, and any person being in possession of it either as a pledge or security for debt or without lawful authority or excuse is liable under section 156 (9) of the Army Act to a fine of twenty pounds (£20) or imprisonment for six months, or to both fine and imprisonment."

PROTECTION CERTIFICATE (Officer).

The under-mentioned Officer of the

*Reserve of Officers	... will be *Relegated to the Reserve	Service Category II.
*Special Reserve of Officers...	will be *Disembodied	Service Category III.
*Territorial Force ...	will be *Disembodied	Service Category IV.
*Temporary Officers	...will be *Gazetted out of the Service.	Service Category V.
*Retired Officers re-employed	will cease to be employed...	Service Category VI.
*Militia ...	will be *Disembodied	Service Category VII.

with effect from 26/1/19 unless he hears to the contrary from the War Office, on and after which date he will not be entitled to draw pay. He will be entitled to wear uniform for one week from the above date and upon occasions authorized by Regulations.

†Rank:—

Temporary 2/Lieut

Acting ✓

Brevet ✓

Substantive ✓

Honorary ✓

Surname BULL
(Block letters)

Christian Names ALFRED CHARLES

Permanent Address 27 Dam St
Lichfield

Agent or Paymaster Cox & Co

(Signed) Percy W. Dovell Lt for Lt Col Rank.

Date 25 JAN 191 Commanding No. 3 DISPERSAL UNIT

		Code Number
Dispersal Area No.	VI B	15
‡Theatre of War or Command	Northern	2
§Regiment or Corps to which belonging	3/S Staffs	65
Unit with which last serving	2/S Staffs	
Place of rejoining in case of emergency	CLIPSTONE	15
Occupation in civil life	Wood Carver	
Born in the year	1896	
Medical Category	A1	
Married or Single	Single	

Date Stamp of Dispersal Unit or Disembarkation Office.

Dis o

25 JAN 1919

CLIPSTONE.

* Strike out whichever is inapplicable.
† Substantive rank will be recorded in the case of all but Temporary Officers ; also Brevet, Temporary, Acting or Honorary Rank, whenever such rank is held.
‡ e.g., France, India, Gibraltar, Southern Command, etc.
§ When a Corps is composed of more than one part, the part to which the Unit belongs must be stated, e.g., R.E., 23rd Field Co. ; R.E., 17th Divisional Signal Co. ; A.S.C., H.T., 283 Co. ; A.S.C. M.T., 253 Co.

Showing Alf's new rank of Second-Lieutenant. Document from the collection of the Staffordshire Regiment Museum.

dead German soldier.

Most of the men were very young and very resilient. They had that ability to believe in their own immortality and not enough life experience to consider the moral implications of what they were doing. Many had come straight from school or straight from the factory and had never left their home county before, never mind the country.

19. Bell tents (so called because of their shape) were set up in Rest Camps as temporary accommodation for the men. They provided shelter from the rain but could get bone achingly cold in winter. In the middle of each were often braziers used to keep the chill away. Anything was burnt, wood, coal, etc. As a result the tents were often full of smoke (and still not very warm). The camp that Alfred is describing is a Rest Camp. They were often far from restful. They're often remembered as dirty, cold, and cheerless collections of tents in a muddy patch that had already been churned up by war and the passing through of thousands of men, and where the guns could still clearly be heard. Real rest with decent food, warmth, clean sheets and a view that included a few trees didn't happen unless you were badly wounded enough to be sent home.

20.   Moving forward under cover of darkness to a new defensive position that you had never seen before, and in any case was impossible to pin point as there are no distinguishing features on a blasted battlefield by which to take your bearings, meant that getting lost was very common. It was an extraordinarily dangerous situation to be in as once you had lost all sense of where you were, it was quite possible to be quietly creeping towards the guns of the enemy. Individual men had a great fear of getting lost when sent out on patrol etc. If you were wounded you would not be found, if you were killed your body would just decompose into the mud. There are stories of healthy men simply disappearing into a muddy sink hole and drowning. In some places, trenches were so close that they could effectively join up with the German trenches, only separated by a wall of sandbags! It was imperative that you could read a compass, but in the dark how would that be achieved? It must be one of the greatest miracles of the war that officers and men so often reached their destination.

In 'Twelve Days On The Somme', Sidney Rogerson, an Officer, describes what he wore on the morning that an attack was to take place. "I put on trench boots, donned a heavy cardigan, decorated with woolly mascots, under my khaki jacket, and a leather jerkin above it. Over all I buckled on the various items of my "Christmas Tree" – gas respirator, water bottle, revolver [for officers only] and haversack – took a rolled-up ground-sheet instead of an overcoat, wound a knitted scarf around my neck and exchanged my cap for a 'battle bowler'." The traditional Tommie's helmet was in fact not introduced until 1916, before that only caps or leather helmets were worn. The metal helmet saved countless lives and could also be used as a washing bowl, a candle holder and even as a seat.

Alf during his service in WW2.

When this lousy war is over

When this lousy war is over, no more soldiering for me,
When I get my civvy clothes on, oh, how happy I shall be!
No more church parades on Sunday, No more putting in for leave,
I shall kiss the sergeant-major, How I'll miss him, how he'll grieve!

When this lousy war is over, no more soldiering for me,
When I get my civvy clothes on, oh how happy I shall be.
No more NCOs to curse me, no more rotten army stew.
You can tell the old cook-sergeant, to stick his stew right up his flue.

When this lousy war is over, no more soldiering for me,
When I get my civvy clothes on, oh how happy I shall be.
No more sergeant bawling, 'pick it up' and 'put it down'
If I meet the ugly b*****d, I'll kick his arse all over town.

back. Mason got back and brought four or five small loaves which I broke up among the men. I never had a bit of it myself. This was our second day and night without food or sleep.

We decided that the place in front of us was Pouleux. We were told to make our way back to where we had started from. Here we had rations and time to sleep.

This was where my platoon found some bottles of wine that had been lost or dumped. Mason was blind drunk and I thumped him and threatened him, but could not keep him quiet.

The C. O. sent for me. I told him that I had all the rum I wanted, but they would tell me where it was. Everyone to dug-out except the sentry and his mate. Next morning Lt. Bell was taken to the rum and all was forgiven.

After four days doing working parties with R. E. s we started the long march to Belgium.

While on the Somme for a time we had as our temporary colonel De Wyatt, V.C., one arm and one eye. In the second war he was a brigadier and served in Norway with the para-troopers there. Later he was in the desert with General Robertson. The yarn was that he wanted to be killed in action.

Our march to Belgium finished at Diche Beach, where the lines were very close - we looked back on Regal Hill.

It was after this that I came home for a commission. Pepper soon followed me. When he went out again I heard that he was killed within a week.

My adventures the third time out to France ended the war for me after St. Quentin with a bullet through my left arm at Woraceguin Hill.

First I must explain how I was with Bates and the fourth South Staffs in March, 1918 and the German advance on Paris. I was only in just three days.

When it started to rain shells and machine gun fire 2nd Lt. Bates was roaming round looking for trouble. He did not know the meaning of fear and was a rough merchant.

When I went out the third time we were at Calais together. One day in the mess he came in wearing a couple of medals - the French and Belgian Croix de Guerre. This was the first time I knew him for one of the War Heroes. It turned out he had been recommended for the V.C. three times, the only

medal he wanted but never got.

If anyone was to get into trouble it was to be the expend-ables like Bates and dull. There was trouble with some 51st Division Jocks who refused to go up the line- a little mutiny and they were going to pay a visit to Prove Marshall, who had one of their men in custody. Bates was acting Captain now and he was detailed to stop them. The main road into Calais was over a small bridge and another bridge on a minor road. Why I was put in charge of this second bridge I never knew, but think Bates had something to do with it. Anyway they did not come my way and a Staff Officer took away Bates' Lewis gun. The Jocks went up the line next day like lambs.

Bates and I went up the line to the 5th S. Staffs. The Battalion were in front of Bethune and things were very different from being on the Somme.

A miniature railway took rations up the line and the track was hit by a shell - it was quickly replaced by spares. It was more open country with acres of wheat. This was where we did daylight patrols. An officer and a man were all day in No Man's Land on company fronts.

My first term in the front line was very eventful and gave me confidence which I never lost afterwards.

The relief of the front line company went smoothly, but an hour or so later we got shelled badly . I was at the head of the communcation trench and one of my platoon (a boy about my own age, came scrambling saying he was going home or something. I threatened him and eventually two men sat on him to keep him quiet.

Shelling eased off but there was hell to play on our left and looking over that way about 200 yards I saw a thing that made me laugh. A pack mule had got loose and any time a shell got near him he lay down and then was up and off again.

It was the only time I had a platoon officer in the line. His name was Poizer and I saw little of him - but he was all right and knew his job.

The weather was awful and we wore thigh boots. Rain, snow, frost sometimes. We looked like snowmen covered in rime from top to toe.

September 29th, 1985 Today, 67 years ago the Staffordshire Brigade broke the Hindenburgh Line and brought the first world war end in sight.

Transcripts of Alf's account

The Last Word

It was only 100 years ago, just a blink of an eye.

The jokes of our early 1900s ancestors are still funny. We understand their newspapers, songs and postcards and when we look at photographs, it's a modern individual who gazes back at us. WW1 is still close enough for some of us to have met those who fought in it, there's no gaping chasm of generations between then and now. We've met soldiers of the Great War and shaken them by the hand.

Both my paternal grandfather and maternal great-grandfather fought in WW1. My Father's father joined up by appropriating his brother's birth certificate, which gave his age as 18 rather than the 17 years he could actually claim. As a boy then, if a boy who had already been working in Birmingham's factories for several years, he went to the front. He came back...changed. My Grandfather drank all the remaining years of his life and was a violent bully to both his wife and his children. He carried a ball-bearing in the muscle of his upper-arm that he would sometimes cause to pop to the surface by flexing the muscles in his shoulder. It was one of the few times he tried to be jocular, and even then it was in a rather grim manner. The war, for him, carried on until the 1970s when he died of gangrene poisoning, probably exacerbated by the gas he inhaled in 1917. The impact of that war was felt by everyone he ever came across, as he carried on the battle that still raged in his head.

My Mother's grandfather brought the war home in another way. Kind, thoughtful and tragically short-lived (once again probably due to the influence of his war service), he fought his own demons through a refusal to ever again be barbaric.

We still live every day with the remains of the First World War. It coloured the way that our grandparents and great-grandparents brought up their own children, and how they in turn raised their families. We are a direct result of the carnage and strange glory of that tragic four year struggle.

There has been a lot of public soul searching recently on how best to remember the warriors, whilst lamenting the war. To my mind, we have no right to pity them, as pity diminishes the recipient. Our job is to bear witness to every long hour, every bullet shattered minute and every time a man or woman stood up on legs that shook so much they could hardly carry them.

It is our job to stand with the man on sentry duty through the long, cold night. To sit by the man sleeping in a hole scraped in the earth and to watch, in unflinching solidarity, the terror, exhilaration and grief of these ordinary men doing extraordinary things. These men are not saints, these women are not angels, they're as fallible and susceptible as you and I, but if we take the time to know them, to listen and remember, then we cannot fail to honour them.

The King commands me

to assure you of the true sympathy

of His Majesty and The Queen

in your sorrow.

Kitchener

Further Reading and Acknowledgements

The following books have been invaluable in my research for First Lines.

Twelve Days On The Somme. A Memoir of the Trenches, 1916. By Sidney Rogerson with Introduction by Malcolm Brown. 2006 version published by Greenhill Books/Lionel Leventhal Ltd and MBI Publishing Co.

A Nurse At The Front. The First World War Diaries of Sister Edith Appleton. Edited by Ruth Cowen. Published by Simon and Shuster.

Staffords In The Great War, 1914-1918, A Brief History by Jim Tanner. Published by the Staffordshire Regiment Museum.

Goodbye To All That. By Robert Graves.

Those interested in this subject may also wish to read…

Lichfield in the First World War – The War Diaries of W.E.Pead. Published by The Lichfield Press.

Honours and Awards The South Staffordshire Regiment 1914 – 1919. By J.C.J. Elson. The author of this excellent book is the Head of Research at the Staffordshire Regiment Museum:

My sincere thanks to The Staffordshire Regiment Museum and my publisher Mr Paul Oakley, without whom this book would never have been created.

All care has been taken to ensure, as much as possible, that the letters, documents and photographs within First Lines have been correctly attributed. The opinions of the writers are their own and not necessarily shared by the author or publisher.